THE STRANGE CASE OF
DR JEKYLL
AND
MR HYDE

ROBERT LOUIS STEVENSON

adapted by Adrian Flynn

OXFORD
UNIVERSITY PRESS

Great Clarendon Street, Oxford OX2 6DP

Oxford University Press is a department of the University of Oxford.
It furthers the University's objective of excellence in research,
scholarship, and education by publishing worldwide in

Oxford New York

Auckland Cape Town Dar es Salaam Hong Kong Karachi
Kuala Lumpur Madrid Melbourne Mexico City Nairobi
New Delhi Shanghai Taipei Toronto

With offices in

Argentina Austria Brazil Chile Czech Republic France Greece
Guatemala Hungary Italy Japan Poland Portugal Singapore
South Korea Switzerland Thailand Turkey Ukraine Vietnam

This adaptation of **The Strange Case of Dr Jekyll and Mr Hyde**
© Adrian Flynn 2011

Activity section © Oxford University Press 2011

The moral rights of the author have been asserted

Database right Oxford University Press (maker)

First published in 2011

British Library Cataloguing in Publication Data

Data available

ISBN 978 019 8310716

20 19 18 17 16 15 14 13 12 11

Typeset in India by TNQ Books and Journals Pvt. Ltd.
Printed in Great Britain by CPI Group (UK) Ltd., Croydon CR0 4YY.

Acknowledgements
Artwork by Robin Lawrie/Beehive Illustration

Cover images © kparis/iStockphoto & Dmitrijs Bindemanis/Shutterstock

The Publisher would like to thank Jenny Roberts for writing the Activities section.

CONTENTS

General Introduction

With a fresh, modern look, this classroom-friendly series boasts an exciting range of authors – from Pratchett to Chaucer – whose works have been expertly adapted by such well-known and popular writers as Philip Pullman and David Calcutt.

Many teachers use OXFORD *Playscripts* to study the format, style, and structure of playscripts with their students; for speaking and listening assignments; to initiate discussion of relevant issues in class; to cover Drama as part of the curriculum; as an introduction to the novel of the same title; and to introduce the less able or willing to pre-1914 literature.

At the back of each OXFORD *Playscript*, you will find a brand new Activity section, which not only addresses the points above, but also features close text analysis, and activities that provide support for underachieving readers and act as a springboard for personal writing.

Many schools will simply read through the play in class with no staging at all, and the Activity sections have been written with this in mind, with individual activities ranging from debates and designing campaign posters to writing extra scenes or converting parts of the original novels into playscript form.

For those of you, however, who do wish to take to the stage, each OXFORD *Playscript* also features 'A Note on Staging' – a section dedicated to suggesting ways of staging the play, as well as examining the props and sets you may wish to use.

Above all, we hope you will enjoy using OXFORD *Playscripts*, be it on the stage or in the classroom.

WHAT THE ADAPTER SAYS

Robert Louis Stevenson published his stunning story *The Strange Case of Dr Jekyll and Mr Hyde* in January 1886 as a 'shilling shocker'. It was intended for readers who liked to curl up by the fire in the middle of winter, with a thoroughly blood-chilling tale of the supernatural.

It was an immediate success with the public, who were equally thrilled and appalled by the novella's gradual revelation that decent Dr Henry Jekyll and the murderous Mr Edward Hyde were two sides of the same person. It was a simple idea, brilliantly developed by Stevenson. As a result, his story is regarded, alongside 'Frankenstein' and 'Dracula', as one of the foremost works of horror fiction ever written.

Although it has been adapted many times for the theatre, cinema and television, it still presents significant challenges to an adapter. Thanks to the story's lasting success, most contemporary audiences know that Jekyll and Hyde are the same person, before the drama begins. As a result, it's impossible to recreate the shock the first readers must have felt on reaching the story's astonishing conclusion. The novella is also rather short to make into a full-length play.

Another problem is that much of the plot is revealed in two long written documents, rather than described when it is actually happening. A strictly faithful dramatisation would therefore spend much of its time with the characters sitting down, reading out letters; not the most exciting sort of theatre. There are also no major female characters in the original. None of this is a criticism of Stevenson's wonderful tale, which succeeds exceptionally well as a novella; simply a recognition that an adapter has work to do, if a play based on it is going to succeed in a modern-day classroom or youth theatre.

To address these difficulties, a number of liberties have been taken with Stevenson's text. Several of the female roles have been made more significant, and one or two new ones invented. Mr Utterson's male clerk has become Miss Guest, and been given a subplot of her own. Poor Sir Danvers Carew, who merely popped into the original in time to be murdered, has been fleshed out as a very hypocritical member of parliament. Perhaps most remarkably, Dr Hastie Lanyon, who dies of shock in the original story, has been spared an early death in the adaptation, so that he can play an important part in the play's final scene.

None of these alterations has been made lightly. The new material is simply intended to echo Stevenson's central theme of the constant battle in human nature, between our highest aspirations and our more basic urges. How many people in public life today might wish that, like Henry Jekyll for a time, they could keep up a respectable public appearance, while their wildest desires took on a different form, to be satisfied well away from the eyes of the press and the paparazzi?

As with all the adaptations in this series, the play is intended to be suitable for performing onstage, as well as to be read in the classroom. I also hope it will encourage people who haven't yet read Stevenson's original work to look at it and discover for themselves what a splendid 'shilling shocker' it still is.

Adrian Flynn

A Note on Staging

If you're creating a set for this version of *Dr Jekyll and Mr Hyde*, it may help to remember the story's main theme: the stark contrast between what we make public about ourselves and what we choose to keep hidden. Lighting, sound and scenery may all be used to emphasise this duality, with the shadows, darkness and fog of night-time Victorian London occasionally punctuated by lighter, sunnier moments in Utterson's office and the day-time streets.

The play has been written with an upper and a lower level to the stage in mind, dividing the public area of Jekyll's house from the private chamber where he conducts his experiments. An upper level would also allow Emma Kay to look down on the murder at the end of Act 1. Other settings, such as Utterson's office and Doctor Lanyon's house, should be established as simply as possible, with one or two furnishings which can easily be carried on and off without disrupting the flow of the action. Everything onstage should contribute in some way to a growing sense of horror as the story unfolds.

The greatest challenge in any production will depend on how the central roles are cast. If Jekyll and Hyde are played by two separate actors, the full transformation scenes may literally depend on smoke and mirrors, with a switch of actors made through a full-length looking-glass, for example. Having two different actors would also allow for some imaginative interpretations of duality: a Jekyll and Hyde of different races or sexes, for example.

A single actor taking on the challenge of both roles will have to find his or her own individual method of transforming, so that an audience's jaw drops. I suspect the key to this may lie in well-defined changes of movement, posture and voice, rather than ducking behind the scenery to pull on a giggle-inducing mask or wig.

However, anyone brave enough to put this on stage is likely to be far more inventive and imaginative than I am, and will probably come up with some much better solutions. So I won't add anything else, except...

Good luck and have fun!

COSTUMES AND PROPS

Act 1

Scene 1   On the upper level: cabinet stocked with glass phials, beakers and other items used in experiments; a skeleton or skull hanging on the wall; a bell-rope attached to the wall. On the lower level: a tall free-standing mirror; large table (with a drawer) and four chairs.
Supper things (finished) for four people and drinking glasses
Brandy decanter
Cheeseboard
Trolley
Key
Measuring beaker, a paper of powder and glass phial with liquid in

Scene 2   Two desks with a typewriter on one of them
Papers (legal documents and papers for the typewriter)
Pens
Large legal document for Sir Danvers Carew
Filing cabinet/drawers

Scene 3   Banknote

Scene 4   Old-fashioned/Victorian gaslight, near to a door off an 'alley'
Tray of matches with strap for hanging around the neck
Enfield's walking stick
Overcoat for Enfield with collar
Cigar
Hyde's wallet
Two £5 old-fashioned bank notes
Key (the same as used in Act 1, Scene 1)
Cheque

Scene 5   Office props as in Act 1, Scene 2; Jekyll's handwritten will

Scene 6   Street props as in Act 1, Scene 4
Street sellers' goods; trays, teapots and china ornaments; snails; onions and asparagus (sparrow grass); eel pies and sheep's trotters; Enfield's walking stick

Scene 7	Crystal vase
Scene 8	Street props as in Act 1, Scene 4
	Key (the same as used in Act 1, Scene 1)
	Hyde's address card
Scene 9	No additional props needed
Scene 10	Main office props as in Act 1, Scene 2
	Jekyll's/Hyde's lion-head walking stick
Scene 11	Main medical rooms props as in Act 1, Scene 1
	Four drinking glasses for Jekyll and his guests
	Two decanters of brandy
	Jekyll's/Hyde's lion-head walking stick
	Laboratory notebook
	Measuring beaker, a paper of powder and glass phial with liquid in
Scene 12	Large broom
	Coin (half a crown)
	Jekyll's/Hyde's lion-head walking stick (with the lion-head handle becoming detached in the fight)
	Representation of a window

Act 2

Scene 1	Newspapers for vendors
	Small coins for pedestrians
	Representation of a window
	Sir Danvers Carew's large legal document (from Act 1, Scene 2)
Scene 2	Main medical rooms props as in Act 1, Scene 1
	Jekyll's/Hyde's broken walking stick (with the lion-head handle missing)
	Measuring beaker, a paper of powder and glass phial with liquid in
	Pen and paper
Scene 3	Burned remains of Hyde's chequebook
	Apron for Mrs Huggett
	Lion-head handle from Jekyll's/Hyde's walking stick

Scene 4	Main medical rooms props as in Act 1, Scene 1 Newspapers for vendors Used beaker, a paper for powder and glass phial Hyde's letter
Scene 5	Main office props as in Act 1, Scene 2 Jekyll's handwritten will Hyde's letter
Scene 6	Main medical rooms props as in Act 1, Scene 1 Large umbrella Jekyll's overcoat
Scene 7	Main office props as in Act 1, Scene 2
Scene 8	A park bench
Scene 9	Armchair Newspaper Letter
Scene 10	Armchair as in Act 2, Scene 9 Small drawer from Jekyll's medical cabinet containing phial of liquid and paper of powder Measuring glass
Scene 11	No additional props needed
Scene 12	Main medical rooms props as in Act 1, Scene 1 Packet of chemical salts
Scene 13	Armchair as in Act 2, Scene 9
Scene 14	Main medical rooms props as in Act 1, Scene 1 Paper and pen Broken key (similar to the one used in Act 1, Scene 1) Tools (mallet and chisel) Jekyll's letter

CHARACTERS

DR JEKYLL'S HOUSEHOLD

Dr Henry Jekyll	A highly qualified and respected doctor in Victorian London
Mr Edward Hyde	Dr Jekyll's alternative self *(Both parts could be played by one actor)*
Poole	The butler
Mrs Temple	The housekeeper
Bradshaw	The coachman
Tump	The footman
Housemaid 1	
Housemaid 2	

OTHERS

Mr Gabriel Utterson	A lawyer and long-standing friend of Dr Jekyll
Miss Guest	Mr Utterson's legal clerk
Mr Richard Enfield	Mr Utterson's cousin
Mr Gray	A college friend of Mr Enfield
Sir Danvers Carew	A respected MP and client of Mr Utterson
Celeste	A close friend of Sir Danvers Carew
Dr Hastie Lanyon	A friend to Dr Jekyll and Mr Utterson
Kitty Huggett	The landlady of disreputable lodgings
Emma Kay	A housemaid who witnesses the murder
Inspector Newcomen	A Scotland Yard detective

MINOR PARTS

Ann Manning — A young match-seller
Mr Manning — Ann's father
Mrs Manning — Ann's mother
Jenkins — Dr Lanyon's butler
A police constable
A crossing-sweeper
Newspaper vendors 1, 2, 3
Street sellers 1, 2, 3, 4

ACT 1

SCENE 1

Evening. Dr Jekyll's medical rooms.

A door at the top of some steps leads to a partially visible upper level where a cabinet is stocked with glass phials, beakers and other items needed for chemical experiments. A skeleton, or skull, hangs on one wall.

A lower level has a tall, free-standing mirror in one corner.

*In this part of the room, **Dr Jekyll, Mr Utterson, Sir Danvers Carew** and **Dr Lanyon** are finishing supper round a large table.*

***Poole,** the butler, stands discreetly to one side, waiting to serve brandy. **Mrs Temple,** the housekeeper, puts a cheeseboard on the table.*

Jekyll	A dissecting room, gentlemen! Fifty years ago, human corpses were cut up and investigated in here.
Carew	How extraordinary, Jekyll.
Jekyll	That's why the room seemed so fitting for my housewarming. Think of the advances in medical knowledge it has witnessed.
Lanyon	I assume one of the former owners was a doctor?
Jekyll	Indeed. The same as you and I, Lanyon. He worked at a time when it was extremely difficult to acquire dead bodies for research. Legally, anyway.
Carew	You mean he used bodysnatchers?
Jekyll	So I believe. The fruits of newly made graves were dug up and brought to the back door in the still of night. *[He points offstage, then realises that **Mrs Temple** is taking a great interest in the conversation]* That will be all, Mrs Temple.
Mrs Temple	Yes, sir.

14

Utterson	It was a delightful meal.
Mrs Temple	Thank you, Mr Utterson. I try to oblige.
	Mrs Temple, intrigued, leaves the room as slowly as possible, as the conversation resumes.
Carew	So there's quite a history to this place?
Jekyll	Indeed, Sir Danvers.
Carew	No need of formality! We were all students together, long before I entered parliament and was knighted. Call me Carew, as always.
Jekyll	Very well, Carew. I am told the bodysnatchers used a special knock. Once admitted from the yard, they carried in the lifeless bodies, wrapped in rags. Within minutes, spleens, hearts, lungs and livers were sliced up to reveal their secrets. On this very table!
Utterson	Thank you for mentioning it so soon after the beef roulade.
Lanyon	Come now, Utterson. A lawyer should be made of sterner stuff.
Utterson	I'm afraid any moment, you and Jekyll will produce scalpels to find out exactly what I am made of. *[Beckons to Poole]* Brandy, Poole.
Poole	Sir.
	Poole pours Mr Utterson a brandy.
Carew	Why buy such a macabre house, Jekyll?
Jekyll	There's nothing macabre about it. It's ideal. My consulting-rooms open onto a respectable street. My patients needn't fear being seen there. Back here, by the yard and alley, I have the privacy I crave to continue my own researches.
	Carew holds his glass out for Poole to fill, but doesn't look as the servant fills the glass.
Utterson	Do you mean to cut up bodies as well?

Jekyll	Far from it. My interests are of a more… spiritual nature.
Carew	In what way?
Jekyll	*[Wanting privacy]* You may leave now, Poole.
Poole	Very good, sir. *[**Poole** leaves briskly]*
Jekyll	*[Confidentially]* Gentlemen, I'm not interested in how muscle and bone connect… I am engaged in dissecting the human mind.
Carew	*[Puzzled]* Dissecting the human mind?
Jekyll	I mean to tear apart the different sides of a man's personality. The good from the bad. The cowardly from the brave.
Lanyon	What nonsense, dear chap.
Jekyll	Far from nonsense! I appeal to Utterson's dry legal mind. *[To **Utterson**]* You must agree, the various parts of a man's soul affect his body? For example, anger reddens his face? Fear makes his heart beat more strongly?
Utterson	Well, yes. That's simply common sense.
Jekyll	And so is what I propose. To cut apart these different aspects. The way we cut, say, a diseased foot from a healthy leg.
Lanyon	What an absurd fancy! *[To **Carew** and **Utterson**]* He was just the same when we were students. Full of useless imaginings.
Jekyll	*[Angry]* Useless? No, sir! If I achieve what I set out to do, you and Carew'll be more pleased than anyone.
Carew	Why?
Jekyll	We are all men of standing, aren't we? Respected in the world for our professional skills. Our upright natures?
Carew	I believe the world looks on us pretty favourably, yes.
Jekyll	Yet, behind our public faces lie shadows. We each have pleasures, wishes, dark desires we don't necessarily want others to know about.

Utterson	*[Interrupts]* Jekyll, really!
Lanyon	This isn't a matter for polite conversation.
Jekyll	No? All I'm suggesting is a man may rise far higher, if he can cut out the animal side of his nature.
Lanyon	We are all made the same way. No one can take the beast out of a man.
Jekyll	I mean to find a way.
Lanyon	My dear Jekyll, what utter nonsense!
Carew	I have to agree with Lanyon.
Lanyon	You can no more separate a man's passions from his intellect than you can … well … create a unicorn from the salts and spirits you play with upstairs. *[**Lanyon** gestures in the direction of the upper level]*
	***Carew** and **Utterson** laugh*
Jekyll	*[Furious]* I do not play with them! And as for not succeeding… *[He's on the point of saying more, but stops himself. With a great effort, he disguises his temper]* Hmm! You're right. Good company and wine have made me babble on. I apologise.
Utterson	No need. We're all friends since practically childhood, aren't we?
Carew	Indeed. And, with that familiarity in mind, may I also speak openly?
Lanyon	You usually do.
Carew	All this talk of animal passions has – for some reason – brought Madame Cuvier's establishment to mind.
Lanyon	*[Laughs]* Dear Madame Cuvier.
Carew	Why don't we round off this delightful housewarming by going on there for a hand or two of cards? And perhaps a cigar?
Utterson	Is that all you have in mind, Carew?

Carew	I understand two of Madame's nieces have recently arrived from Paris. Who knows? They may wish to join us at the card table.
Jekyll	I've never known anyone with so many nieces.
Carew	Surely it would be rude not to say 'Comment t'allez-vous?' to the dear girls? *[Stands up]* Anyone joining me?
Lanyon	I'm all for improving Anglo-French relationships. *[Stands up]*
Carew	Utterson?
Utterson	Not me, thank you.
Lanyon	I imagine you'll spend the rest of the evening with a dusty book of law?
Utterson	Quite possibly.
Carew	Jekyll?
Jekyll	No. I've work to get on with. And visiting Madame Cuvier is not to my taste.
Carew	What? You hypocrite, Jekyll!
Jekyll	*[Jumps up]* I am no hypocrite!
Utterson	*[Trying to make peace]* Gentlemen!
Carew	You're full of humbug. You enjoyed women's company as much as any of us at university.
Lanyon	You did, Jekyll! For all you tried to keep it secret.
Jekyll	That is unfair…
Carew	*[Cuts in]* Oh, stop being so high and mighty! You're no different from the rest of us…
Utterson	*[Cuts in]* Carew, Lanyon, may I suggest you leave now? Who knows if Madame Cuvier's nieces will remain unattached, if you wait much longer.
Lanyon	Very true.

Utterson	Go and enjoy your hand of cards. Jekyll and I will finish our brandy together.
Carew	Very well. Good night, Jekyll. *[Holds out his hand]*
Jekyll	*[He shakes **Carew**'s hand very briefly]* Sir Danvers. *[He nods at **Lanyon**]* Lanyon.
	***Jekyll** turns away as **Lanyon** is about to offer a handshake.*
Carew	*[Moving away]* Come on. We should hurry.
Lanyon	*[Following]* Do you know these young ladies' names yet?
	***Carew** and **Lanyon** go.*
Utterson	Well? A final toast to your new home?
Jekyll	I am no hypocrite, Utterson.
Utterson	I know you're not.
Jekyll	I've never denied – even when I was a student – that I'm the same as other men. I'm not ashamed of my passions. They are as much a part of me as anything else. But from the outset of my career, I have wanted to be a success. To be well known and respected for my work. Is that so deplorable?
Utterson	Far from it.
Jekyll	To ensure no breath of scandal ever harms my public standing, I have learned to conceal my pursuit of certain pleasures.
Utterson	I believe it's the common way of doing things.
Jekyll	But oh, what a waste of effort, this constant war between my rational mind and primitive instincts. If only these two natures could be separated, I might know some peace.
Utterson	If you can't find a medical solution to your problem, I recommend the law, Jekyll.
Jekyll	The law?
Utterson	We lawyers are buried under so much paperwork, we don't

	have time for any pleasure. In fact, there's a matter I should be attending to now, if you can spare me?
Jekyll	Willingly. We both have work to do, despite the lateness of the hour.
Utterson	I noticed your laboratory already prepared, though you've barely moved in.
Jekyll	Thank you for helping me celebrate the move. *[Shakes Utterson's hand warmly]* You, at least, have been excellent company tonight.
Utterson	I've enjoyed myself greatly. And hope to see you again very soon.
Jekyll	You will. Good night, Utterson.

*Mrs Temple comes into the room with two **housemaids**.*

Utterson	*[Leaving]* Good night, Jekyll. Good night, Mrs Temple. A wonderful meal.
Mrs Temple	Thank you again, sir. Girls, busy yourselves.

*The **housemaids** load all the supper things onto a trolley as **Mrs Temple** goes to speak with **Jekyll**.*

Sir?

Jekyll	What is it? I haven't time to discuss domestic matters.
Mrs Temple	No, sir. *[Discreetly]* I simply wondered if you mean to go out again later?
Jekyll	*[Quiet, but angry]* How is that any of a housekeeper's business?
Mrs Temple	It's only that I'm a light sleeper, sir. And I heard you returning in the early hours last night.
Jekyll	*[Embarrassed]* You have the hearing of a bat, Mrs Temple.
Mrs Temple	Mr Poole and I are afraid we may lock the door to the yard one night, without realising that you are out... *[Tactfully]* ... taking the night air.

Jekyll	You have a key to the yard?
Mrs Temple	*[Takes key out]* Here, sir.
Jekyll	*[Takes key]* I shall assume full responsibility for it from now on.
Mrs Temple	Very good, sir.
Jekyll	Forget the door exists.
Mrs Temple	Yes, sir.

Jekyll	Now, I have a great deal of work to do. So if you and the young ladies have finished clearing…
Mrs Temple	Certainly sir. *[Moves away]* Come on girls.
	Mrs Temple and the **housemaids** *gather up the last of the supper things and start going offstage with the trolley.*
Jekyll	Thank you, Mrs Temple.
Mrs Temple	*[Going offstage]* I'm happy to oblige, sir.
Jekyll	*[Watches her leave, then sarcastically repeats]* 'Happy to oblige'!

He runs up the stairs to the upper level of the rooms.

'Happy to oblige'! The shame of it!

He addresses the skeleton, as he takes a paper of powder and a phial of liquid from the cabinet.

Do you hear? My housekeeper makes notes on when I leave and when I come back from seeking a little friendly company. How humiliating!

He mixes the powder and liquid in a beaker.

Well, no more. I won't 'take the night air' in my own guise ever again. I can't put my good name at risk.

He holds the beaker up, then turns towards the skeleton.

Sssh! Be quiet. *[Laughs at his own joke]* Still, you're better company than Doctor Lanyon. He was a pompous prig at university and even more pompous tonight. Think I can't separate a man's passions from his intellect, Lanyon?

He comes down the steps, glances at the mirror, then drinks the contents of the beaker, which taste revolting. **Jekyll** *coughs and splutters, then gradually regains self-control. He puts the empty beaker down on the table and speaks with great disappointment.*

A twelfth attempt. A twelfth failure. One last packet of salts from a new supplier to try. If that doesn't activate the phosphorus and ether mix, I will have failed. Utterly.

Jekyll *goes offstage. Lights down on his medical rooms.*

SCENE 2

The next morning. Mr Utterson's office.

Lights up on **Miss Guest**, *who is typing at a desk.*

Utterson *comes onstage.*

Utterson	The codicil to the Macfarlane will?
Miss Guest	*[Takes sheet of paper from typewriter]* Ready to be added, Mr Utterson.
Utterson	*[Takes document]* Thank you. *[Glances at it, then puts it down]* The lease for the property in Devonshire Street?
Miss Guest	*[Holds up another document on her desk]* Drawn up and ready for both parties' attention.
Utterson	*[Takes and glances at document]* You are extremely efficient, Miss Guest.
Miss Guest	Thank you, sir.

Utterson	*[Puts leasing document down]* Then we are finished for the morning?
Miss Guest	Not quite. Sir Danvers Carew sent a note earlier. He intends calling in shortly.
Utterson	Did he say why?
Miss Guest	No, sir. Only that he would appreciate your prompt, professional attention.
Utterson	And he shall have it. Though I don't understand why he didn't say something last night.
Miss Guest	He was at Dr Jekyll's housewarming as well, sir?
Utterson	Yes. Though he and Jekyll had something of a falling out.
Miss Guest	How unfortunate.
Utterson	There was an odd atmosphere to the whole evening. I do wish Jekyll had taken another house.
Miss Guest	Is this one badly built?
Utterson	No. But it was once the haunt of bodysnatchers and anatomists.
Miss Guest	Good heavens.
Utterson	I'm afraid my friend's already eccentric nature may be further disturbed by such morbid surroundings. *[The office door opens offstage]* Ah, that'll be Carew.
	Richard Enfield *walks onstage.*
Miss Guest	He is very much changed then.
Utterson	*[Pleased]* Richard! I took you for someone else.
Enfield	Apologies. I wouldn't normally come to your offices, Gabriel. Have I called at a bad time?
Utterson	Not at all. *[Introducing them to each other]* Miss Guest, this is the cousin I've spoken of on many occasions. Mr Richard Enfield. Richard. My senior clerk, Miss Guest.

Enfield	*[Very taken with her. Bows his head]* Pleased to meet you, Miss Guest. *[Pause]* Tell me, do you have a first name?
Miss Guest	Indeed I do, sir.
Enfield	I'd be charmed to know what it is.
Miss Guest	I shall remember that, sir. In case I ever wish to see you charmed.
	*She feeds a new sheet of paper into the typewriter and starts to type whilst **Utterson** and **Enfield** talk.*
Utterson	*[Amused]* You'll have to try much harder to win Miss Guest's favour, Richard.
Enfield	*[Intrigued]* Will I, indeed?
Utterson	Now, have you come for advice on a legal matter?
Enfield	No, no. This is purely personal. I'm afraid I can't have supper with you on Thursday after all.
Utterson	What a pity.
Enfield	An old college friend is passing through London. If I don't meet him then, I may wait an age for another opportunity.
Utterson	Well, never mind. I quite understand.
Enfield	But will we still have our usual walk on Sunday?
Utterson	I depend upon it, Richard. *[The office door opens offstage]* It's the only exercise I get these days.
	*Sir Danvers Carew comes onstage. **Miss Guest** stops typing.*
Carew	I'm here, Utterson. And I can't spare much time.
Utterson	Good morning, Carew.
Enfield	*[To **Utterson**]* I see you're busy. I'll take my leave.
Utterson	Very well, Richard.
Enfield	Till Sunday. *[He nods to **Carew**]* Good day, sir.
Carew	Good day.

Enfield	*[Quietly to* **Miss Guest**_]_ I shall discover your name yet.
	He goes out. **Miss Guest** *takes the sheet out of the typewriter and starts writing notes on it.*
Utterson	My clerk says you wish to see me on a legal matter, Carew.
Carew	Yes. Something quite delicate, but... *[He takes* **Utterson's** *arm and leads him away from the desk]*... a small point first.
Utterson	What's that?
Carew	You know I'm not the sort to give myself airs and graces, don't you, Utterson?
Utterson	Indeed not.
Carew	Calling me Carew last night, amongst friends – all well and good. Perfectly proper.
Utterson	*[Starts to understand]* Ah...
Carew	But in public, eh? Before strangers?
Utterson	I fully understand, Sir Danvers.
Carew	Since Her Majesty went to the trouble of knighting me – no sense letting the title go to waste, eh?
Utterson	Of course not, Sir Danvers. Now, the... er... legal matter?
Carew	*[Embarrassed]* Ah... as I say, it's very delicate. *[He looks over his shoulder to check* **Miss Guest** *is busy working. He then speaks quietly]* You may recall, after leaving Jekyll's housewarming, Lanyon and I went on to... er... Madame Cuvier's?
Utterson	You hoped to meet her nieces, I recall.
Carew	We most certainly did. And we weren't disappointed. One of them in particular is a most delightful girl. Celeste. Very sweet-natured.
Utterson	I'm glad you found such pleasant company.
Carew	Yes! Though, oddly enough, she didn't take much notice of me at first.

Utterson	*[As though surprised]* No?
Carew	But then – soon after I'd mentioned some recent trifling successes on the stock market, I think – she came up to me. And shyly confessed she'd been completely smitten with me from the outset.
Utterson	What a charming girl.
Carew	Exquisite. The trouble is, I don't want to leave such a fresh, young thing lodging at Madame Cuvier's.
Utterson	No?
Carew	Absolutely not. All sorts of riff-raff goes there. In fact, I promised Celeste I'd set her up in a nice little apartment of her own as soon as possible.
Utterson	I see.
Carew	Purely out of a protective instinct, you understand?
Utterson	Naturally, Sir Danvers.
Carew	Only now, I'm starting to worry about my promise.
Utterson	For what reason?
Carew	In case the press – or my political opponents – hear about it. A Member of Parliament paying for an attractive young woman's accommodation? It could be misinterpreted.
Utterson	Very possibly.
Carew	There'd be an almighty scandal. I can't let that happen.
Utterson	Certainly not, Sir Danvers.
Carew	So I wondered... Is there any way I can purchase an apartment for Celeste without my name appearing anywhere in the transaction?
Utterson	Well...
Miss Guest	*[Looks up from her work]* Oh, that's quite straightforward, sir.
Carew	*[Horrified]* You've been listening?

ACT 1 SCENE 2

Miss Guest	It's hard to ignore such a gifted public speaker, Sir Danvers.
Utterson	Don't worry. Miss Guest is the soul of discretion.
Miss Guest	*[Takes a large document from a drawer and brings it to **Carew**]* Perhaps you might like to take this home and complete it at your leisure.
Carew	*[Takes the document. Surprised]* There's a standard form for this type of thing?
Miss Guest	Oh yes, sir. We get the same request from a great many MPs.
	Lights down on Utterson's office. **Utterson, Carew** *and* **Miss Guest** *go offstage.*

● ●

SCENE 3

Two days later. A street in Soho. The doorway of Kitty Huggett's lodging house.

Lights up on **Jekyll** *and* **Kitty Huggett.**

Jekyll	*[Holding a large banknote in his hand]* You understand the arrangement, Mrs Huggett?
Kitty Huggett	Indeed I do, sir.
Jekyll	My friend, Mr Edward Hyde, will lodge in your rooms. But, for the moment at least, I shall be responsible for all payment. Is that acceptable?
Kitty Huggett	If I might see the note, Dr Jekyll? *[Jekyll gives her the banknote. She looks at it with great satisfaction]* Very acceptable, sir.
Jekyll	Good. And I should make it clear that my friend is a very private person.
Kitty Huggett	Is he, sir?
Jekyll	He doesn't want a landlady who watches when he comes in and goes out. Or listens at the door.
Kitty Huggett	Oh, I would never do that, sir.

Jekyll	And he cannot bear neighbours who ask questions or pry into his affairs. Will he be free from such nuisances here?
Kitty Huggett	*[Knowingly]* Isn't that the very reason you're renting lodgings in this part of London, sir? *[She laughs]* Do we look the sort of people who care what our neighbours get up to?

Jekyll looks at her and their surroundings with some disgust, then nods and walks offstage.

*Lights down on **Kitty Huggett**.*

• •

SCENE 4

Two nights later. A street with an alley running offstage. A locked door on the alley leads into Dr Jekyll's backyard.

A gaslight illuminates part of the street.

***Ann Manning**, a young match-seller, with a tray of matches round her neck, stands and shivers under the gaslight.*

***Richard Enfield**, carrying a stout walking stick, comes on with his friend **Gray** at the opposite side of the stage.*

Enfield	We must split up here, Gray. *[Points in the direction of the gaslight]* I'm heading this way.
Gray	I'll see if I can find a cabbie to take me to Dalston.
Enfield	You'll be lucky this late.
Gray	Then it'll be footwork, all the way. It was good to meet up, Enfield.
Enfield	We'll see each other again at your wedding. What a wonderful surprise that was.
Gray	Why not bring the intriguing young lady you mentioned with you? Miss... who was it?
Enfield	Miss Guest.

Gray	Miss Guest! With that name, she's fated to accept the invitation.
Enfield	I shall try to persuade her.
Gray	Good luck. *[Puts his hand out]* And good night.
Enfield	*[Shaking **Gray's** hand]* Good night, dear fellow. *[**Gray** goes offstage]* Enjoy your last weeks of freedom.
	*Left by himself, **Enfield** turns up his collar against the cold. He fishes in his overcoat pockets for a cigar, as he mutters to himself.*
	Miss Dora Guest... Miss Emma Guest... Miss Eliza Guest?
	*He puts the cigar in his mouth, then pats his pockets for a light. **Ann Manning** sees him.*
Ann Manning	*[Calls]* Excuse me, sir! Do you need a match?
Enfield	Indeed, yes. How fortunate you're working this late.
Ann Manning	Not fortunate, sir. I stand here sixteen or more hours every day. You stay there, sir. I'll come to you. The road is filthy from horses.
	*Just as **Ann Manning** starts to cross towards **Enfield**, **Edward Hyde** hurries onstage.*
Hyde	Out of my way, girl!
	He swings his arm, sending her and the match-tray sprawling on the ground.
	Damn you! You've made me step in the dirt.
	*He starts stamping on the match-tray. **Enfield** hurries across.*
Ann Manning	Help!

Enfield	You, sir! Stop there!
Hyde	Why in blazes should I?
Ann Manning	Oh, my arm!
Enfield	*[Raises his walking stick threateningly]* Because I command you to.
	Doors open offstage. There are cries of 'What's happening?', 'What's the row for?', 'Can't you let people sleep?', etc.
Hyde	Use violence on a defenceless man, would you?
Enfield	As you have used it on this poor girl! Unless you stay where you are.
Ann Manning	*[Sits up, feeling her arm]* How it hurts.

Mr Manning	*[Coming onstage]* It sounds like our Ann.
Mrs Manning	*[Coming onstage]* What's happened to you, girl? *[Comforts her daughter]*
Ann Manning	That man hit me!
Mr Manning	Then I'll hit him.
Enfield	*[Steps between **Hyde** and **Mr Manning**]* Stand back, sir. Don't let hot blood lead to worse.
Hyde	*[Half fearful and half defiant]* I am perfectly innocent. Your daughter stepped into my path without looking.
Ann Manning	He hit me! Then stamped on the tray.
Enfield	All quite deliberately.
Mr Manning	*[To **Enfield**]* Let me deal with this, sir. Look away and you need never know what happens.
Enfield	We are not animals. We will put this right through the law.
Mrs Manning	He's a toff. No policeman'll take my girl's word against his.
Hyde	No, they won't. Because I am telling the truth. It was an accident.
Enfield	*[To **Hyde**]* What is your name, sir?
	Hyde *doesn't answer.*
	I asked your name.
Mr Manning	I'll empty his pockets. There'll be something there to identify him.
Hyde	*[Defiant]* I am Mr Edward Hyde.
Enfield	I saw what happened, Mr Hyde. And never mind who the police believe. If you don't make proper reparation to this poor child, I'll raise such a stink about your name, you'll have to leave London.
Hyde	I see what you're about. Very well. *[He takes out a wallet]* No gentleman likes to be the subject of a scene. *[He takes out two*

*banknotes and offers them to **Mr Manning**]* Here's ten pounds to stop your daughter's mewling.

Mr Manning	*[Disgusted]* Ten pounds!
Hyde	It's all I have about me.
Mr Manning	You've destroyed her stock. She won't be able to work for weeks. Fifty pounds to make up the damage!
Mrs Manning	If her arm is broke, she may never work again. A hundred pounds!
Hyde	*[To **Enfield**]* Well, sir? Do you mean to let them fleece me?
Enfield	They have suffered the loss, not I. They must decide.
Hyde	In that case, I see I am helpless. But I have a friend lives close by. *[He points to a door a little way from the gaslight]* If I go through the yard, I'm sure he will advance me the rest of the money.
Enfield	Then please do so.
Hyde	It will only take a moment. *[He takes out a key and lets himself through the doorway]*
Mr Manning	What are the chances he'll lift himself over the wall and run off?
Enfield	Then see that he doesn't.

Mr Manning nods, then goes to stand in the doorway, looking offstage. Enfield goes to Ann Manning, who is getting up with her mother's help.

How are you, my girl?

Ann Manning	My arm's a little better, sir. But I'm so shook up.
Mrs Manning	She's very grateful. We're all grateful you took her part against that monster.
Enfield	It wouldn't be necessary if you didn't let your daughter work alone so late.
Mrs Manning	What else can we do, sir? We have six other mouths to feed, as

well as hers. At least match-selling is honest labour. There's others her age have much worse ways of making money.

Enfield   Yes. You are right. Forgive me for being so quick to condemn.

Mr Manning   *[Coming back from the doorway]* He's coming back.

*Hyde comes out of the doorway. He holds a cheque out to **Mr Manning**.*

Hyde   There's your blood money.

Mr Manning   *[Disgusted]* A cheque! *[To **Enfield**]* Can you see if it's in order, sir? Me and the wife never had time for reading and writing.

*Enfield takes and inspects the cheque under the gaslight, then turns to **Hyde**.*

Enfield   *[Surprised]* This is the friend you call on in the middle of the night?

Hyde   Yes. Hasn't he signed his name clearly enough?

Enfield   Oh, it is perfectly clear, Mr Hyde. *[Reads]* It has been made out by Dr Henry Jekyll.

Lights down. Everyone goes offstage.

SCENE 5

> *The following day. Mr Utterson's office.*
>
> *Lights up on **Utterson**, who is showing **Miss Guest** a hand-written legal document.*

Utterson The most extraordinary document, isn't it? Hand-written.

Miss Guest By Dr Jekyll?

Utterson He's had to draw it up himself. He knows any sane lawyer would refuse to do it for him.

Miss Guest It does seem most unusual, sir.

Utterson It's entirely without logic or sense. I've known Jekyll nearly all his life. He's never spoken of the man before.

Miss Guest *[Inspecting the will]* Yet if he dies, he means to leave everything to this stranger.

Utterson Which is unsettling enough. *[Turns off a page in the will]* But this is even more bizarre.

Miss Guest *[Reading]* '… in the event of my disappearance or unexplained absence for more than three calendar months, all my possessions, including my house, are to pass into the hands of my friend and benefactor, Mr Edward Hyde.'

Utterson 'Unexplained absence'! Why on earth should Jekyll worry about suddenly disappearing?

Miss Guest I've no idea, sir.

Utterson I tried persuading him not to lodge such an eccentric will with me, but he insisted.

Miss Guest Did he say who Mr Hyde is?

Utterson Jekyll told me nothing. Except that he is a very dear friend.

Miss Guest He must be.

Utterson	I'm surprised – worried, even – that Hyde has taken such a hold on Jekyll, in such a short space of time.
	The office door opens offstage.
	File it carefully, Miss Guest. Only we must know of its existence.
Miss Guest	Sir.
	Miss Guest files the will in her desk as Enfield hurries onstage.
Enfield	Gabriel, apologies for disturbing you again.
Utterson	You are always welcome, Richard. But I see you're agitated.
Miss Guest	Should I fetch some brandy?
Enfield	No thank you. I need advice, not spirits.
Utterson	What's happened?
Enfield	I witnessed something awful last night. I fear it concerns one of your closest friends.
Utterson	Who? What happened?
Enfield	I can show you, if you have time.
Utterson	I'll make time. *[To Miss Guest]* Will you deal with anything that arises in my absence?
Miss Guest	Certainly, sir.
Utterson	Then let's be off, Richard. It seems I am to have a morning of troubling experiences.
	Utterson and Enfield hurry offstage. Miss Guest looks quizzically after them.
	Lights down on the office. Miss Guest goes offstage.

SCENE 6

A few minutes later. Lights up on the street and alley with a door leading to Dr Jekyll's backyard.

Street sellers, with goods to sell, and pedestrians cross the street.

Street seller 1   *[Calling]* Teapots and china ornaments. Get your teapots and china ornaments.

Street seller 2   *[Calling]* Snails for your cage-birds, two and six a pail. Snails for your cage-birds.

Street seller 3   *[Calling]* Get your vegetables here! Onions and sparrow grass. Cheapest prices in London. Onions and sparrow grass.

Street seller 4   *[Calling]* Eel pies and sheep's trotters. Eel pies and sheep's trotters.

The street sellers repeat their cries as they move across the stage, perhaps one or two of them stopping to make sales to the pedestrians.

Enfield enters with Utterson.

Enfield   I was astonished to see the signature on the cheque.

Utterson   Do you know Jekyll?

Enfield   By sight alone. We've never been introduced, but I recalled you've sometimes mentioned him as a friend.

Utterson   A most valued friend.

Enfield   That's what I thought. So I can't understand why he's on close terms with such a vicious man.

Utterson   Yet the cheque proved good?

Enfield   Yes. The father of the unfortunate girl and I took it to the bank this morning. I was certain it couldn't be genuine. But it was accepted without quibble.

Utterson   And where did Hyde fetch the cheque from?

Enfield	*[Points to the door near the gaslight]* There.
Utterson	That gateway leads into the backyard of Jekyll's new home. Did Hyde knock, or call for a servant to let him in?
Enfield	No. He had his own key.
Utterson	What? Are you sure, Richard?
Enfield	I saw him open the door with it.
Utterson	That is disturbing. *[Confidentially]* Strictly between ourselves, Jekyll was already acting a little strangely at his housewarming. I feared some slight brain disorder, brought on by his new surroundings. But if he gives open access to someone who strikes down a child…
Enfield	Quite brutally.
Utterson	…then I'm afraid there's something worse at the root. Tell me, what does Hyde look like?
Enfield	I can see him in my mind's eye now. But it's damnably hard to describe him.
Utterson	Try, Richard. Much may rest on it.
Enfield	He seemed quite young. But not innocent. There was something downright detestable about him. I never saw a man I disliked so much. But I can't say why, except that he was somehow… badly made… It's no good! I can do no better than that.
Utterson	*[Very discreetly]* Did he resemble Jekyll in any way?
Enfield	I didn't notice a likeness. But then, I didn't search for it. I couldn't bear looking at the man.
Utterson	Pity.
Enfield	*[Realises what **Utterson** is thinking]* You think Hyde might be Jekyll's son? Born out of wedlock, and now he's blackmailing his father?

Utterson	I've said no such thing, Richard. And neither must you. To anyone.
Enfield	I swear I won't.
Utterson	There may be some quite straightforward reason for Jekyll befriending Hyde. But I confess, at the moment, I fear my friend is in some danger from the brute you describe.
Enfield	*[Holds up his walking stick]* I was glad to have this with me last night. Otherwise I believe Hyde would have attacked me.
Utterson	I wish Jekyll had such a stout means of defence.
Enfield	That's easily remedied. I'll order another from Marshall and Snelgrove, if you like. You can let him have it as a belated housewarming present.
Utterson	What an excellent idea. Would you mind?
Enfield	Not at all. I only live ten minutes from the shop.
Utterson	Thank you, Richard. That at least will provide some protection. But perhaps the best way to defend Jekyll, is to talk with Hyde myself. Work out what kind of man he really is.
Enfield	How will you find him?
Utterson	By looking. All over London, if needs be. Though, if he visits Jekyll regularly, it will be as well to come back here from time to time. If he be Mr Hyde, I shall be Mr Seek.

Lights down. **Utterson**, **Enfield**, *and any remaining* **street sellers** *and* **pedestrians** *go offstage.*

• •

SCENE 7

A few days later.

Lights up on the hallway of Dr Jekyll's house.

Mrs Temple *is cleaning a crystal vase, while she talks to* **Poole**.

Mrs Temple	Dr Jekyll has become a great deal more secretive lately, hasn't he? And it's all that man's fault.
Poole	It's not our place to say, Mrs Temple.
Mrs Temple	Admit it, Mr Poole. You don't like Hyde any better than the rest of us.
Poole	[*Correcting her*] Mr Hyde. If our master considers him a fitting companion, who are we to judge differently?
Mrs Temple	I tell you, he's a real odd fish. Cold and clammy. Just looking at him gives me the shivers.
Poole	I confess there is something a little unsettling about his appearance.
Mrs Temple	What about his voice? It turns my bones to jelly! And the way he comes and goes in the back rooms, as though he owns them.
Poole	Nevertheless, the master must see qualities in him that we don't. They wouldn't be friends otherwise.
Mrs Temple	The doctor can't like Mr Hyde that much. You never hear them talking together, do you?
Poole	Well, no.
Mrs Temple	Or see them go out in each other's company.
Poole	I've noticed Dr Jekyll goes out a great deal less often than he used to.
Mrs Temple	That's true. Especially at night. He doesn't creep in and out like a tomcat any more.
Poole	[*Disapprovingly*] Mrs Temple!
Mrs Temple	[*Sarcastically*] Perhaps he lets Mr Hyde do his sinning for him.

Lights down. **Poole** *and* **Mrs Temple** *go offstage.*

SCENE 8

*An evening soon after. The street and alley, with the doorway into Jekyll's backyard. The gaslight comes up on **Utterson**, who is blowing on his hands to keep warm.*

***Hyde** comes onstage, heading for the alley.*

Utterson	*[Approaches him]* Mr Hyde, I think.
Hyde	*[Flinches, then regains his self-control]* That's my name. What do you want?
Utterson	I'm Mr Utterson. An old friend of Dr Jekyll's. I saw you making for his door and wondered if you might let me in.
Hyde	What for?
Utterson	To see him.
Hyde	You won't find him in. He's not at home.
Utterson	Oh. You sound very confident of his movements?
Hyde	*[Taking out his key]* Yes, I am.
Utterson	Might I ask, is that because you're lodging with him now?
Hyde	No, I'm not. Though how the devil does that concern you? *[Puts the key in the lock]*
Utterson	Who knows? I may need to find you one day, Mr Hyde. On a legal matter perhaps.
Hyde	*[Remembering the will]* Possibly. *[He takes an address card from his pocket]* This is where I live. *[He gives **Utterson** the card]* You won't know it. It's in Soho.
Utterson	I'll have to step over to read it. *[He stands under the gaslight]*
Hyde	*[Suspiciously]* How did you know my name?
Utterson	Would you be kind enough to come into the light yourself, Mr Hyde?
Hyde	What for?

Utterson	Knowing your address will be of little use, if I can't recognise your face another time.
Hyde	Very well. *[He joins **Utterson** in the gaslight]* But you haven't answered my question.
Utterson	*[Looking closely at **Hyde**]* One moment, please. *[Finishes looking]* I see you're not family.
Hyde	*[Angrily]* How did you know my name?
Utterson	That's no mystery. I was given your description.
Hyde	Who by?
Utterson	Does it matter? We have mutual friends.
Hyde	*[Aggressively]* Do we?
Utterson	Jekyll, for instance.
Hyde	Hah! You're a liar!
Utterson	Come now. That's not fitting for a gentleman.
Hyde	And neither is lying. *[He moves offstage and opens the door into the backyard]* Jekyll never told you about me! Hah!

Hyde goes offstage through the gate.

| Utterson | *[To himself]* Why does Jekyll have dealings with such a savage? I mean to get to the heart of this. |

Utterson hurries offstage.

Lights down on the street and alley.

• •

SCENE 9

A minute later. Lights up on the hallway of Dr Jekyll's house. The doorbell rings.

Poole enters.

Poole	*[Comes onstage, muttering to himself]* No need to pull the bell off the rope! *[He opens the front door to* **Utterson**] Good evening, sir.
Utterson	*[Coming in]* Good evening, Poole. Is your master in?
Poole	I'm afraid not, sir.
Utterson	That's what I thought. Yet a moment ago, I witnessed Mr Hyde go in by the door to the old dissecting rooms.
Poole	Very possibly, sir.
Utterson	Is that supposed to happen, while Dr Jekyll's away?
Poole	Oh yes, sir. It's quite normal now.
	Mrs Temple appears at the edge of the hallway and stops to listen.
Utterson	Your master clearly places a lot of trust in that young man.
Poole	Yes sir, he do indeed. We all have instructions to obey him.
Mrs Temple	*[Coming in]* That's right, sir. He can order us about, however he pleases.
Poole	*[Quietly]* Mrs Temple! Haven't you work to attend to?
Mrs Temple	*[To* **Utterson**] Of course, we're all happy to obey. Since that's what the master chooses.
Utterson	*[Confidentially]* And what sort of a man is Mr Hyde? I only ask, because I've never met him here socially.
Poole	Oh you wouldn't do, sir. Mr Hyde never dines with Dr Jekyll.
Mrs Temple	We see very little of him, this side of the house. He mostly scurries around by the laboratory. With that odd sort of walk of his. Like an ape, almost.
Poole	*[Interrupting]* Mrs Temple, I believe you said the preserving pans need some attention.
Mrs Temple	But...
Poole	The sooner they're seen to, the better.
Utterson	I shan't keep either of you from your duties any longer.

Jekyll	*[Coming onstage]* I thought I heard your voice, Utterson.
Utterson	My dear Jekyll! You *are* here.
Jekyll	I'm sorry if you were informed otherwise.
Poole	*[Puzzled]* I must apologise, sir. I could have sworn you were out.
Jekyll	Clearly I wasn't. Now, about your business, both of you. I will see Mr Utterson out.
Poole	*[Leaving]* Very good, sir.
Mrs Temple	*[Leaving]* Sir.
	Mrs Temple and **Poole** exchange puzzled glances as they go offstage.
Utterson	I wish to talk with you urgently, Jekyll.
Jekyll	Not tonight, I'm afraid.
Utterson	It's a most pressing matter. About the true character of your friend Edward Hyde
Jekyll	*[Sharply]* I don't wish to know!
Utterson	*[Offended]* I see.
Jekyll	*[More conciliatory]* I've been busy today, that's all. I'm simply too tired, otherwise I would enjoy speaking with you.
Utterson	Really?
Jekyll	Yes, of course. But it must wait a day or two. You are coming to my soirée on Friday? Carew and Lanyon will be there as well.
Utterson	I'm not sure.
Jekyll	Please. I'll be rested by then. Much more myself. I'll listen carefully to whatever you have to say.
Utterson	*[Appeased]* Very well, then. Till Friday.
	Lights down. **Jekyll** and **Utterson** go offstage.

SCENE 10

The following Friday afternoon. Mr Utterson's office.

*Lights up on **Miss Guest** working, at her desk. **Enfield** is trying to interest her in the new walking stick.*

Enfield	Good, stout mahogany. Beautifully turned.
Miss Guest	*[Continuing to work]* Indeed, Mr Enfield.
Enfield	A brass ferrule. And what do you make of the lion-head handle?
Miss Guest	Very impressive.
Enfield	*[Piqued]* You're not the least bit bothered, are you?
Miss Guest	I've promised to give it to Mr Utterson as soon as he returns. I'm not sure what more you expect of me.
Enfield	You could show some interest, Miss Guest. It's a fine piece of handiwork. Solid and dependable. A little heavy and old fashioned perhaps. But worth your attention, nonetheless.
Miss Guest	Are we still discussing the walking stick?
Enfield	Now you're trying to make a fool of me.
Miss Guest	Not at all, Mr Enfield. I never attempt to improve on nature.

*Annoyed, **Enfield** steps away for a moment, while **Miss Guest** carries on working.*

Enfield	*[After regaining his self-control]* I shan't give up, you know? When I set myself a task, I stick at it.
Miss Guest	So I'm beginning to realise.
Enfield	*[Trying to guess her name again]* Beatrice? Catherine? Dodie?
Miss Guest	*[Drily]* Are we to work our way through the whole naming dictionary?

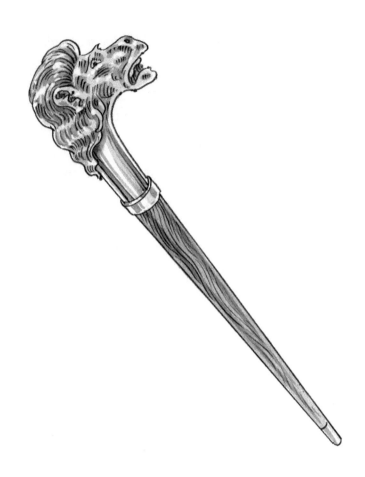

Enfield	Not if you tell me your first name voluntarily.
	Miss Guest starts typing a new document. Enfield sighs.
	I've discovered one thing about you already, Miss Guest.
Miss Guest	*[Typing]* Is that so?
Enfield	My cousin tells me you are a keen student of handwriting.
Miss Guest	*[Typing]* It's the nature of my job to see a wide range of styles. Naturally I've developed one or two thoughts on the matter.

46

Enfield	He says you have a very sharp eye. You can pick out even the smallest details that would elude the casual observer. He claims you can often identify the author of an unsigned document.
Miss Guest	*[Typing]* I believe I have some small gift for doing so.

Enfield *suddenly crouches by* **Miss Guest,** *causing her to stop typing.*

Enfield	And yet you can't read the simplest message, writ large on a man's face.
Miss Guest	I believe I can read it very well, Mr Enfield. You are not the first of Mr Utterson's connections to show an interest in a female clerk.
Enfield	I'm not some tired old rake, 'showing an interest'! Normally, I'm the last person to force myself on a lady's attentions. But… *[Sighs. Gets up]* Oh, I'm sorry. You're right. I am being obnoxious.
Miss Guest	*[Sincerely]* No, Mr Enfield. You're not. *[Pause]* Perhaps I'm even a little flattered by your attention. But I simply know better than to trust it.
Enfield	Why not trust me? *[He lays the walking stick on the desk]* I'm as solid and true as this. I swear, I'm just as I seem.
Miss Guest	You may well be, Mr Enfield. But I have witnessed many people come through these doors. And I have learned that almost every man – and woman for that matter – has at least one dark secret to hide.

Lights down on **Miss Guest,** *who takes the walking stick, as she and* **Enfield** *go offstage.*

Later that evening. Dr Jekyll's medical rooms. Lights up on a small drinks party.

Poole *and* **Tump,** *the footman, stand discreetly to one side, filling glasses when needed.* **Jekyll** *and his guests,* **Utterson, Lanyon** *and* **Carew** *are standing in pairs.*

While **Jekyll** *talks to* **Lanyon, Carew** *steers* **Utterson** *away from them, so that he can speak in private.*

Carew	Is everything going ahead smoothly?
Utterson	With the apartment?
Carew	Ssh! Ssh! Ssh!
Utterson	They're too deep in medical matters to take any notice, Sir Danvers.
Carew	*[Correcting* **Utterson***]* Carew! While we're in private, Carew is perfectly acceptable.
Utterson	Very well, Carew. All that remains is for you to look over the final document I gave you when we met outside.
Carew	*[Patting his breast pocket]* Still safely here.
Utterson	If you're satisfied with these last terms and conditions, my office will move ahead to rent the apartment on your behalf.
Carew	And my name will be completely hidden?
Utterson	Absolutely.
Carew	I shall read the document as soon as I get home. Then return it to you, first thing tomorrow.
Utterson	I shall act as soon as I receive it.
Carew	In fact, I may go home at any moment. Jekyll's been poor company all evening. Lost in another of his distant moods.
Utterson	He does seem distracted.

Carew	Let's see if Lanyon's been able to talk any sense into him.
	*Carew and **Utterson** join the others.*
Lanyon	I suppose I should be pleased, Jekyll.
Jekyll	You sound thoroughly pleased. Some might say 'smug', even.
Lanyon	Well, it is something of a feather in my cap. Being able to number such illustrious names amongst my latest patients.
Jekyll	I wish you much joy of them.
Lanyon	But I can't be fully happy, knowing that I've taken two of them from your lists.
Jekyll	You needn't concern yourself.
Carew	What's this Lanyon? Market fluctuations in the doctoring business?
Lanyon	One or two well-placed ladies have recently started consulting me. At Jekyll's expense I'm afraid.
Jekyll	Don't worry. I can spare you the odd duchess or two.
Carew	What's the matter, Jekyll? Are you losing the healing touch? Forgotten how to waft round the smelling salts?
	Lanyon laughs.
Utterson	It's surely not right to make fun of a man's professional difficulties.
Jekyll	I'm in no difficulties!
Lanyon	One of the ladies – I couldn't possibly give her name – says she had great trouble seeing you recently, Jekyll. She claims you have become erratic in calling on your patients.
Jekyll	Because I have more important demands on my time.
Lanyon	More important than caring for the sick?
Jekyll	Yes!
Lanyon	You don't mean the tomfoolery you mentioned the last time we were here?

Jekyll	I am too busy to humour idiotic old women, with nothing better to do than imagine they've contracted the latest, fashionable illness.
Carew	Oh, come now, Jekyll. That's no way to talk.
Jekyll	I shall talk as I please in my own home.
Carew	Have the sense to listen to a close friend, who has your best interests at heart. These experiments Lanyon refers to…
Jekyll	What of them?
Carew	Forget them until you have put your practice in good order again.
Lanyon	That's good advice, Jekyll.
Jekyll	I haven't asked for advice.
Carew	But I am giving it anyway. The way I would throw a drowning man a rope, whether he requested it or not.
Utterson	Jekyll's no drowning man.
Carew	He soon will be professionally, if he doesn't put himself on dry land again.
Lanyon	I'm afraid that's true.
Jekyll	Nonsense!
Carew	Losing patients so you can waste time on absurd theories? It makes you seem directionless. As though you don't know where you're going.
Jekyll	Hah!
Lanyon	Carew has a point.
Carew	Word'll soon spread you're not a doctor to rely on. And, as we've agreed, reputation is all-important. Lose that and you've lost everything.

Utterson	Gentlemen! The last time we met ended in hot words. We mustn't let the same thing happen again.
Jekyll	It's all right, Utterson. I'm no more offended by Carew's maunderings than by the wailing of a cat.
Carew	*[Offended]* Well, I've done my best to make you see reason. Since I can do no more, perhaps it's time I left.
Jekyll	*[Glad to see him go]* If you must.
Lanyon	It's growing late for me as well.
Jekyll	Good night to both of you.
Carew	Good night.
Lanyon	And thank you for another… thought-provoking evening, Jekyll. Good night, Utterson.
Utterson	Goodbye gentlemen.
Jekyll	*[To Poole and Tump]* Find their coats.
Poole	Sir.
Utterson	And Poole? Can you bring the package I left in the hall?
Poole	Certainly, sir.
	***Poole** and **Tump** go offstage.*
Lanyon	*[Going offstage, to Carew]* Shall we call on Madame Cuvier again?
Carew	*[Going offstage]* Not I, Lanyon. I've more important matters to attend to.
Jekyll	*[Wryly to Utterson]* Aren't you offended enough to leave as well?
Utterson	I'm used to your ways, Jekyll. Though it's clear your mind is troubled tonight.
Jekyll	No more than has become usual.
Utterson	If you're worried about something, perhaps I can help.

Jekyll	I don't think so, Utterson.
Utterson	At least hear me out. You know my purpose in coming this evening was to speak with you about Mr Edward Hyde.
	Jekyll signals Utterson to be quiet as Poole comes on with the lion-head walking stick.
Poole	*[Offering it to Utterson]* Sir.
Utterson	Thank you, Poole.
Jekyll	Tell Mrs Temple to clear the room tomorrow. I don't want to be disturbed again tonight.
Poole	*[Going offstage]* Yes, sir.
Utterson	*[Holds the walking stick out to Jekyll]* This is for you, Jekyll.
Jekyll	*[Surprised]* A walking stick?
Utterson	A belated housewarming gift.
Jekyll	*[Puzzled]* Thank you.
Utterson	Apart from encouraging you to take exercise, it may also provide some small degree of protection against Hyde.
Jekyll	*[Laughs with disbelief]* I'm meant to turn this on Hyde?
Utterson	He is a violent man. I've heard abominable things about him. And meeting him did nothing to change my opinion.
Jekyll	Yes. I know that you have met. *[He puts the walking stick down]* Isn't it a little forward of you, Utterson? Spying on my friends?
Utterson	I wanted to meet him for your sake. He is a monster, Jekyll. My cousin saw him strike down a defenceless young girl. He would have done her great harm, if he hadn't been prevented.
Jekyll	I don't care to hear about it.
Utterson	You must hear. You, after all, pay for his crimes.
Jekyll	What do you mean by that?

Utterson	I know about the cheque you gave him. If he discovers you are leaving him everything in your will, he may well be tempted to harm you...
Jekyll	[Interrupts] Thank you, Utterson. That is enough.
Utterson	Not till I have made it clear. I can see you are in trouble. And I wish to help.
Jekyll	[Pause. More calmly] My dear Utterson. This is downright good of you... I admit I am in a strange situation as regards Hyde. Painfully situated, even.
Utterson	Jekyll, you know me. I am a man to be trusted. Tell me in confidence what hold this man has over you and, with the law's help, I shall make you free again. I have no doubt of it.
Jekyll	Thank you, Utterson. I would trust you more than any man alive. But it's simply one of those affairs that can't be mended by talking. [Tries to smile] And perhaps matters are not as bad as you imagine.
Utterson	No? Then tell me how they stand.
Jekyll	To put your mind at rest, I will tell you one thing. The moment I choose, I can be rid of Mr Hyde.
Utterson	You swear to that?
Jekyll	I give you my hand on it. [He holds his hand out to **Utterson**, who shakes it] I know you will keep these matters private.
Utterson	Naturally.
Jekyll	But since we are speaking of Hyde – for what I hope is the last time – there's something I want you to understand. I take a great interest in the poor chap. I know he was rude when you met him...
Utterson	[Cuts in] I'm not worried about that.
Jekyll	...But if I am taken away before my time, I want you to ensure he receives what is rightfully his.
Utterson	All your possessions?

Jekyll	Exactly as is stipulated in the will.
Utterson	But my dear Jekyll…
Jekyll	*[Cuts in]* If you knew the facts, Utterson, I'm sure you'd agree to it. It would be a great weight off my mind if you promised to do so.
Utterson	I can't pretend I shall ever like him.
Jekyll	I don't ask that. I only ask for justice. Help him, if and when I am no longer here to do so.
Utterson	*[Considers for a moment. Reluctantly]* Very well. I shall look out for him.
Jekyll	*[Shakes **Utterson's** hand again]* Thank you. For your promise. *[He picks up the walking stick]* And your fine gift. *[He brandishes the stick]* With your friendship, I am protected from all catastrophes.
Utterson	I hope so, Jekyll.
Jekyll	Go home with an easy mind, old friend.
Utterson	It is a little easier, perhaps. Good night, Jekyll.
Jekyll	Good night.

Utterson *goes offstage.* **Jekyll** *looks at himself in the mirror for a moment.*

Should I have told him? The real secret of Edward Hyde? *[He moves away from the mirror and goes up the steps to the upper level]* Ten days ago perhaps I might have spoken. I'd've astounded all of them. Utterson, Lanyon, Sir 'Damned Directionless' Danvers Carew. *[He addresses the skeleton]* Gentlemen, I have done what I said. I have created a potion which completely separates the animal spirit from the man. Gives it a life of its own. What do you think of that? *[Laughs bitterly]* Up to ten days ago, the separations always worked smoothly. *[He takes his laboratory notebook from the cabinet and opens it]* But then?… The laboratory record shows I took no potion that fateful day. I went to bed as myself. Yet when I woke up the next morning, a lean, knuckly hand was lying on the coverlet. The muscles standing out like cords. I had become Hyde without choosing to do so. *[Addresses the skeleton]* You're right. I changed back again, simply enough, didn't I? A single measure of salts, phosphorus and ether. And nothing untoward has happened since then. Maybe I have been worrying for no reason. *[He takes a paper of powder, a beaker and a phial of liquid from the cabinet as he continues to speak]* I must have made some simple mistake in the mixture the time before. Some residue of transformational powder still lay in my blood when I went to sleep. *[To the skeleton]* Quite right. A slight overdose. Nothing more. Hyde is the servant. Not the master. He doesn't come unbidden. *[He starts mixing the powder and liquid in the beaker as he walks back to the stairs]* And it is cowardly of me to wait so long to summon him back. After letting Lanyon and Carew strut and preen all evening, I am due a little pleasure of my own. *[He stops at the bottom of the stairs. Worried]* What if it wasn't a mistake? What if my other self shook loose his fastenings unaided?… Preposterous! Am I to give up my investigations, because of one slight mishap? *[He walks to the mirror]* No. I'm not going to jump at shadows like Utterson. I must carry on until my work has been perfected. *[He toasts himself in front of the mirror]* Your health, sir!

Jekyll drinks the contents of the beaker. His whole body is racked with agonising pain as he transforms into Hyde.

Hyde   *[Ecstatic]* Ten days? That wasn't kind, Jekyll. But now at last I'm freed from my cage.

Lights down on Hyde/Jekyll, who go offstage.

SCENE 12

An hour or so later. Dim lights up on a foggy street in Soho.

Carew walks onstage, arm-in-arm with **Celeste**.

Carew	It really is time I went home, Celeste. My wife will be wondering where I have got to.
Celeste	*[In French accent]* How disappointing, Sir Danvers.
Carew	But don't worry. *[Pats his breast pocket]* I have a document here that will solve all our problems. Once I have returned it to my lawyer.
Celeste	How wonderful.
Carew	We won't have to meet in miserable hotels any more. We'll have our very own love-nest.
Celeste	How often will you visit me there?
Carew	I know you'd like me to be with you every day.
Celeste	Of course, Sir Danvers.
Carew	But I'm afraid I'll only be free to see you once or twice a week. The rest of the time you'll be all on your own.
Celeste	How very disappointing… Still, I expect I will manage.
Carew	Now, shall I walk you back to your aunt's?
Celeste	Please, no. I know my own way from here. *[Points]* And Westminster lies that way.
Carew	How quickly you've learned your way around London. *[He looks round to check no one is watching]* How about a parting kiss?
Celeste	*[Coyly]* Oh no. Please let us wait, until we are safe and snug, in my new apartment, Sir Danvers.

Carew	Very well, Celeste. You divine minx.

*Carew waves tenderly as he walks away. **Celeste** waves tenderly back, until **Carew** turns away.*

Celeste	*[Quietly. In her real, British accent]* Thank Gawd for that. *[She goes offstage]*

Carew walks around, getting lost as he looks for street signs.

*A **crossing-sweeper** comes onstage with a large broom.*

Crossing-sweeper	Clear your path across the road, sir?
Carew	*[Relieved]* Ah, young man. Perhaps you can help me find my way.
Crossing-sweeper	Certainly, sir. Are you after a dog-fight, a gin-palace, or just want to see a show?
Carew	Where's the nearest cab-stand? I need to get to Westminster.
Crossing-sweeper	You're well out of your way, aren't you?
Carew	*[Takes out a coin]* Here's half a crown for good directions.
Crossing-sweeper	*[Takes the coin quickly]* Ta... Here, I've seen your face somewhere, haven't I?
Carew	*[Embarrassed]* I very much doubt it, young man. This isn't the type of area I frequent.
Crossing-sweeper	I have seen you! In the paper.
Carew	Impossible!
Crossing-sweeper	You're a Member of Parliament, aren't you? What you doing round here? There's nothing but lusheries[1] out this way.
Carew	How dare you! You're completely mistaken!

1 A 'lushery' was a Victorian term for a low tavern or drinking den.

Crossing-sweeper	I've got it! Sir Danvers Someone, in't you?
Carew	*[Hurriedly moving away]* No. Not at all. You're quite, quite wrong.
Crossing-sweeper	*[Shrugs]* Thanks for the half-dollar[1] anyway. *[He goes offstage]*

Carew, in a panic, walks blindly through the fog.

Carew	Hello! Cabby! Is there a cabby anywhere?

Hyde, carrying the lion-head walking stick, comes onstage and passes Carew.

	You sir! Stop a moment.
Hyde	Who the devil are you, telling me to stop?
Carew	I'm sorry. I don't mean any harm.
Hyde	*[Recognises Carew]* Oh, I know you, don't I?
Carew	You may have seen my face in some magazine or newspaper. But I've lost myself in this damnable fog.
Hyde	*[Delighted]* Lost, are you?
Carew	Utterly.
Hyde	Directionless?
Carew	I don't know where to find a cab-stand.
Hyde	Like a drowning man, then?
Carew	I don't understand you.
Hyde	*[Uses walking stick to point]* Go this way for a cab-stand.
Carew	This way? Thank you.

Carew starts to move offstage. Hyde deliberately trips him with the walking stick.

Hyde	No. Wrong way! *[Points walking stick]* That way! That way!

---

1 A 'half-dollar' was a slang term for half a crown (twelve and a half pence in modern money – worth the equivalent of about £7.00 in Victorian times).

Carew	Have a care, sir.
Hyde	*[Ferociously]* That way!

Carew starts moving offstage again. Hyde steps in front of him and pushes him back with the walking stick.

Not this way! *[He prods Carew repeatedly with the walking stick]* That way! Or that way! Or that way!

Carew	*[Frightened and angry]* What are you doing, sir?
Hyde	Helping a drowning man.
Carew	Leave me alone.
Hyde	I will help. Whether you've requested it or not, Sir Danvers.
Carew	Who are you?
Hyde	*[Grabs Carew's collar]* The man who will drag you to dry land. You mustn't be found wandering through the vice dens of Soho…
Carew	Let go of me!

Emma Kay, a housemaid, opens an upstairs window of a nearby house to see what's happening.

Hyde	…then you'd lose your reputation. And be no one. Hah! Isn't that right?
Carew	Let go! *[He hits Hyde]*
Hyde	Strike me, would you! No sir! This is how you strike!

Hyde beats Carew to the ground with repeated blows of the walking stick, laughing demonically as he does so.

Carew cries out in fear and pain.

Emma Kay looks on in horror as Hyde lands a last violent blow, which knocks the lion-head handle off his walking stick.

Carew slumps down dead.

Hyde stamps delightedly round the body.

Now where's your reputation? You're no one! No one!

Emma Kay's window creaks as she leans against it. Alarmed,
Hyde stops and looks round, though doesn't see her. He hurries
offstage, leaving the walking stick handle behind.

Emma Kay   *[Struggles to find her voice]* Murder... Help... Murder... *[Cries*
out in horror] Murder! There has been a murder!

Blackout

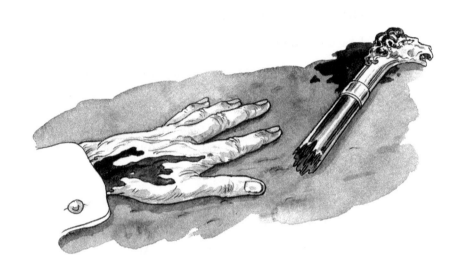

ACT 2

• •

SCENE 1

The next morning. The street in Soho where **Carew** *was murdered. The body and all other signs of the murder have been removed.*

Pedestrians *gossip, pointing out where the murder occurred.* **Newspaper vendors** *cross the stage selling papers.*

Vendor 1	*[Calling]* Shocking murder! Read all about it!
Vendor 2	*[Calling]* Special edition! Man battered to death!
Vendor 3	*[Calling]* Horror in Soho! One penny only.
Vendor 2	*[Calling]* Special edition!
Vendor 3	*[Calling]* One penny only!
Vendor 1	*[Calling]* Read all about it!

Some of the **pedestrians** *buy newspapers as* **Inspector Newcomen** *comes onstage with* **Emma Kay**.

Newcomen	*[Points to the window]* You were up in your room at the time, Miss Kay?
Emma Kay	That's right, Inspector. I'd finished my cleaning duties at last and was hoping to go to bed, when I heard angry voices on the street. So I looked out.
Newcomen	What did you see?
Emma Kay	*[Distressed]* Oh it was awful, sir! I can hardly bear to think of it.
Newcomen	Calm yourself, my girl. This may be vital.
Emma Kay	Well, there was two gentlemen down here. Arguing fiercely.
Newcomen	What about?
Emma Kay	I couldn't make that out, sir. Only that the younger one had the older one by the collar and wouldn't let go. He was a

proper gent, the older one. Nicely dressed. Do you know who he is, sir?

Newcomen	Not yet. His face was beaten beyond all recognition.
Emma Kay	It was such a ferocious attack.
Newcomen	What did his assailant look like?
Emma Kay	It was hard to tell, sir. It was so dark and foggy.
Newcomen	What of his size? His colouring?
Emma Kay	He was quite small. And so wicked-looking, as he lashed out with his stick.
Newcomen	It must have taken considerable force to break the handle clean off... Can you describe his face?
Emma Kay	No better than that, sir. Wicked-looking. He was too far away to give particulars.
Newcomen	Why didn't you call for help at once?
Emma Kay	I tried to, sir. But the sight of that monster, dancing round the other like an ape, froze the wind in my pipes. I couldn't scream. I'm so sorry, sir. It was an 'orrible thing to see. [She puts her head in her hands]
Newcomen	Come, come. You've done well to remember so much.

A police constable comes onstage.

Constable	We've searched the body, sir.
Newcomen	Any identification?
Constable	Just this, sir. [He produces the legal document **Carew** had in his jacket] It doesn't name the murdered man, but it's addressed to his lawyer.
Newcomen	[Takes and looks at the document] A Mr Gabriel Utterson. Let's see what he knows.

Lights down. Everyone goes offstage.

SCENE 2

The same morning. Lights up on Dr Jekyll's empty medical rooms.

A key turns in a lock and a door opens offstage. An ecstatic **Hyde** *comes in, with the broken walking stick.*

Hyde [*To himself*] Safe! I am safe!... It was a bold stroke to go to Mrs Huggett's first, before returning here. But now they cannot catch me. [*He hurries up the steps*] Because I have the most perfect hiding place in the world. [*He takes a paper of powder, a beaker and a phial of liquid from the cabinet as he continues to speak*] After this, I am gone. Vanished from the earth. Like Carew. [*He leaves the powder, beaker and phial of liquid on the cabinet, and turns to the skeleton*] I've sent you a companion in the after-life. Dispatched with all haste. [*He comes down the stairs and strikes the air violently with his broken walking stick and laughs*] What a feeble gift this was! Broke apart after a couple of light blows. [*He throws the walking stick down in disgust, then has a worrying thought*] I shouldn't have left the handle on the street, though. No, no. That was foolish! That interfering imbecile of a lawyer may hear of it. Recognise his gift. Start pestering weak-minded Jekyll for information about his daring friend, Mr Hyde. [*He goes back up to the cabinet and picks up the beaker, phial and paper of powder, which he carries down the steps to the table*] Yes, I'll use you to escape. [*He puts them down on the table*] But not just yet. [*He takes a pen and some paper out of a drawer in the table*] First I must pen a few words to put Jekyll in the clear... [*He sits down*]...and keep that fool Utterson off my scent.

Hyde starts to write, as the lights come down. He goes offstage.

SCENE 3

Later the same morning. A street in Soho. Outside Kitty Huggett's lodging house. There is a loud knock on a door, then lights come up *on **Inspector Newcomen** and **Utterson,** who are waiting to be let in.*

Newcomen	You have been doubly useful to the police, Mr Utterson. Firstly, identifying the body.
Utterson	Poor Carew. To have been so horribly mutilated.
Newcomen	Your second service has been leading me to these lodgings.
Utterson	The maid's description leaves little doubt, Inspector. 'Wicked-looking.' 'Moved like an ape.' I shall be astonished if Edward Hyde doesn't prove to be the murderer.
Newcomen	Where has the woman got to?
Utterson	Shall we knock again?
Newcomen	No need. The curtain twitched back the first time. She knows we are here. *[Calls]* Answer the door, Mrs Huggett. We have seen you are at home.
Utterson	She's no friend to the police, I take it?
Newcomen	Few on this street have any liking for the law.
Utterson	If Hyde is the murderer, I hope there's proof in his room. I'm afraid the maid's evidence, seen at a distance through darkness and fog, will carry little weight in a courtroom.
Newcomen	We found something else by the body which may clinch matters.
Utterson	Oh?
Newcomen	*[Reaches into his pocket]* This…

*A door opens offstage and **Kitty Huggett** bustles on. **Newcomen** takes his hand from his pocket.*

	At last, Mrs Huggett.
Kitty Huggett	I never hurry to hear bad news. And that's all you rozzers ever bring.
Utterson	You have a lodger we are interested in. A Mr Edward Hyde.

Kitty Huggett	*[Intrigued]* Is he in trouble?
Newcomen	There are some questions I'd like to put to him.
Kitty Huggett	You've come to the wrong place, then. The viper cleared out overnight.
Utterson	Are you sure?
Kitty Huggett	See for yourselves, if you like. He's burned all his papers and left his room bare.
Utterson	*[To **Newcomen**]* He must've realised you'd be on to him.
Kitty Huggett	If you catch up with the scoundrel, I hope you make him suffer.
Newcomen	What do you have against him, Mrs Huggett?
Kitty Huggett	He's a foul thing.
Newcomen	I haven't heard you speak like this before.
Kitty Huggett	I don't pretend me and my friends are all sweetness and hymn-singing, Mr Newcomen. But your Mr Hyde was a different sort of badness altogether. Vicious. If you wished him so much as good day, he'd snarl back as though he wanted to kill you.
Newcomen	I don't suppose he's left a photograph of himself?
Kitty Huggett	Not likely. He had a face would break any camera.
Newcomen	Pity. Putting his likeness on a handbill would speed his arrest.
Kitty Huggett	I told you. There's no papers or nothing else left. Except this. *[Takes the burned remains of a cheque book from her apron]* The end of a chequebook I hooked out of the ashes.
Newcomen	I'll take that. *[He takes it from her and looks at it]*
Kitty Huggett	You're welcome to see his room, if it helps put him behind bars. Or, better still, at the end of a rope.
Newcomen	No need. I'll accept your word there's nothing there, Mrs Huggett.

Kitty Huggett	Then I'll say 'good day'. It don't do your health good round here to be seen talking to peelers.

Kitty Huggett goes offstage.

Utterson	You trust what she said without looking at the room yourself, Inspector?
Newcomen	I'll come back if I need to. But her hatred of Hyde seems genuine. I'll swear she's not covering for him.
Utterson	I agree.
Newcomen	And now we have two reasons to hope he'll soon be captured. Money is life-blood for a man on the run. If Hyde has burned his chequebook, he must go to a bank to draw funds. I'll set men to wait and watch at all the main ones.
Utterson	And your second reason for hope?
Newcomen	Ah, yes. *[He takes the lion-head handle out of his pocket]* The handle of the walking stick used to kill Sir Danvers.
Utterson	*[Recognising it]* Good heavens!
Newcomen	A beautiful thing to be used for such a foul purpose, isn't it? Someone may remember seeing Hyde with it on another occasion. If we can show he owned it, it will go badly against him in court.
Utterson	*[Trying to keep his composure]* But it's a common enough handle, isn't it, Inspector? Several men may own such a walking stick.
Newcomen	*[Amused]* Oh, I don't expect it to satisfy a lawyer's sceptical mind by itself, Utterson. But you may be certain – this walking stick points a long way towards our murderer.

Lights down on **Newcomen** *and* **Utterson,** *who go offstage.*

SCENE 4

An hour later. Dr Jekyll's medical rooms and nearby streets.

*Lights up on **Jekyll**, sitting exhausted in a chair by the table on the lower level of his rooms.*

***Newspaper vendors** cross the front of the stage.*

Vendor 1   *[Calling]* Special edition! Murder victim was Member of Parliament!

Vendor 2   *[Calling]* Heartless killer identified!

Vendor 3   *[Calling]* Police seek Edward Hyde.

*The **newspaper vendors** repeat their cries until they've gone offstage.*

***Jekyll** wearily stands up and picks up the empty beaker, phial and powder paper from the table. He goes up the steps to the upper level as he speaks.*

Jekyll   Dear God, what have I done! Carew was a fool and an ass. But to kill him on such feeble provocation. *[He puts the empty phial, beaker and paper into the cabinet]* Though I must be fair to myself. I did not kill him. It was the other. Hyde. Acting like a

madman. Each time he is released, he is stronger. More overpowering. Well – no more! *[He pulls a bell-rope on the wall]* From now on, only the better side of my nature shall walk free. Hyde must be banished for ever.

Poole enters on the lower level.

Poole	You wanted me, sir?
Jekyll	Tell Tump and the coachman I have a job for them.
Poole	Sir?
Jekyll	My medical cabinet – and everything in it – is to be taken out and destroyed. Smashed beyond repair.
Poole	*[Trying to hide his surprise]* Very good, sir. *[He goes offstage]*
Jekyll	There. It must be so. Hyde is confined for ever. Even he thinks it is for the best now. If he shows his face in public again, he'll be seized by an army of hands and marched straight to the gallows. *[Pause. To the skeleton]* I suppose I should be grateful, shouldn't I? To be forced to live as a good man from now on. Nothing but my patients' well-being to be concerned with… I shall win back my reputation and my list in no time. *[Turns away from the skeleton]* You'll see, Lanyon. They'll flock back to me. *[He goes to the cabinet]* All the same, it's a sad farewell. Never again to taste freedom. Pleasure. To be rid of all this is a very final act. *[Pause]* Perhaps a foolish one. What if Hyde comes again without summoning? What if I wake up once more in his form, not mine? And all the necessary chemicals to transform back are gone?

Bradshaw, the coachman, and Tump come onstage.

Bradshaw	Mr Poole says you want us to break up your cabinet, sir?
Jekyll	*[Making a decision]* No, no.
Tump	That's what he said, sir.
Jekyll	I've changed my mind. All it needs is a good strong lock, so that it can't be easily or carelessly opened. See to it during my consulting hours this afternoon.

Bradshaw	Very good, sir.
	*Bradshaw and **Tump** exchange exasperated looks about their master, then go offstage, as **Poole** comes onstage.*
Poole	Mr Utterson's here, sir.
Jekyll	Now?
Utterson	*[Coming onstage]* I must see you at once, Jekyll.
Jekyll	Welcome. *[Comes down the steps]* That will be all, Poole.
Poole	Sir. *[Goes offstage]*
Utterson	Have you heard the dreadful news? Carew has been murdered.
Jekyll	Yes. The streets are full of nothing else.
Utterson	Hyde is named as the murderer and I have reason to believe he must be. The murder weapon was a lion-headed walking stick. Such as I gave you.
Jekyll	It is possible... he took it from me.
Utterson	Carew was my client, but so are you. I must be certain of what I am doing. Tell me truthfully, Jekyll, are you mad enough to be hiding this fellow?
Jekyll	Utterson, I swear to God I will never set eyes on him again. On my honour, I am done with him. It is all at an end.
Utterson	From your side, perhaps. What of his?
Jekyll	He does not want my help. You do not know him as I do. He is gone. Mark my words, he will never be heard of again.
Utterson	You seem very sure.
Jekyll	I am certain of it.
Utterson	For your sake, I hope you are right. If he is caught and brought to trial, your friendship with him – however innocent – will come to light. You will be ruined in the public's eyes.

Jekyll	I've nothing to fear from Hyde. *[He opens a drawer in the table and takes out the letter Hyde wrote]* See, he wrote this. Perhaps it will allay your fears. *[He gives it to **Utterson**]*
Utterson	*[Briefly scans the letter]* 'I, Edward Hyde, have repaid my benefactor Dr Henry Jekyll for his thousand acts of kindness most unworthily'... He says you had no part in any of his criminal actions.
Jekyll	No. I am entirely innocent.
Utterson	*[Resumes reading]* 'No one need fear any further offences, as I have a sure way of leaving these parts. I will never return.' *[Looks up]* Well, this provides some reassurance.
Jekyll	I can't make my mind up whether to show it to the police or not. Not because I care what happens to Hyde. I'm done with him. But because of the damage it'll do my name. Please, take it. And decide for me.
Utterson	*[Puts the letter in a pocket]* Very well. And, if you're willing to speak openly, there's something else I should like to ask.
Jekyll	Please do.
Utterson	The will you lodged with me, leaving everything to Hyde. Did he dictate it to you?
Jekyll	*[Quietly]* Yes.
Utterson	I knew it. I'm sure he meant to murder you for it. You've had a very narrow escape, Jekyll.
Jekyll	Yes, indeed. But I have learned a most valuable lesson. When you get back to your offices, please destroy the will. Edward Hyde is banished from my life for ever.

*Lights down. **Jekyll** and **Utterson** go offstage.*

Twenty minutes later. Mr Utterson's office.

*Lights up on **Miss Guest**, busy at her desk, and **Enfield** sitting comfortably to one side of it.*

Enfield A terrible business.

Miss Guest Very much so.

Enfield You'd've expected the police to catch the villain by now.

Miss Guest Sadly, many criminals go unpunished.

Enfield Is that so, Alexandra?

Miss Guest gives him a quizzical look.

Not Alexandra?

Miss Guest No.

Enfield If I guess your name correctly, will you accompany me to my friend Gray's wedding?

Miss Guest I don't see the two matters are in any way linked. *[She looks on the desk for a document]*

Enfield *[Automatically he hands her the document]* In my heart, they're linked. Maud.

Miss Guest *[Amused exasperation]* Enough! I'll be Florence or Hannah or Zuleika next!

Enfield Then tell me your real name.

Miss Guest *[Seriously]* Suppose I hold myself back for a reason?

Enfield Do you?

Miss Guest *[With difficulty]* Many people, who perhaps have found peace at a certain point in their life, may have memories of earlier times they do not particularly care to remember. Yet, if they are to be honest when they form a new friendship...

Enfield *[Cuts in]* All I want to know is your name.

Miss Guest	Will you be satisfied, if I tell you?
Enfield	For a while.
Miss Guest	Very well, then.
	The office door opens offstage.
	My given name is…
	Utterson *hurries in.*
Utterson	Ah, Richard, good to see you. But I must ask you to call back some other day.
Enfield	*[Getting up]* Yes, but…
Utterson	Tomorrow, perhaps. Or the day after. But I'm afraid Miss Guest and I have an urgent matter to attend to now. Please, you'll have to go.
Enfield	*[Disappointed]* Very well, Gabriel. I'll call in at a more convenient time.
Utterson	*[Shakes **Enfield's** hand]* Good man. I look forward to it.
	Enfield *looks to* **Miss Guest** *for a last word. She smiles, but says nothing as he goes offstage, and out through the offstage door.*
	Can you find me Jekyll's will, Miss Guest?
Miss Guest	Certainly. *[Opens drawer in desk]* It's here, sir. *[She takes it out]*
Utterson	We have the doctor's permission to destroy it.
Miss Guest	Really, sir?
Utterson	I'm delighted to say my old friend seems completely free of Edward Hyde's malign influence at last. *[He takes Hyde's letter from his pocket]* Here's a letter, exonerating him from any part in Hyde's wrong-doing. You may read it, if you like.
Miss Guest	Thank you, sir. *[She looks at the letter and then the will]*
Utterson	Jekyll wants me to decide whether to show it to the police or not. I can't see any purpose in doing so. It won't help bring Hyde to justice. And may harm my friend.

Miss Guest	*[Puzzled]* Sir, the letter is written by Mr Hyde and the will by Dr Jekyll?
Utterson	That's right. Why?
Miss Guest	I'm struck by how similar they are.
Utterson	In what way?
Miss Guest	*[Points out similarities]* The curve of the loops... the way the cross-strokes rise... both texts are alike on several other points as well.
Utterson	So they are.
Miss Guest	Mr Hyde's is sloped rather differently. Otherwise I'd swear they had been written by the same hand.
Utterson	*[Very worried]* No. Surely that's not possible? Jekyll wouldn't forge for a murderer.

Lights down. **Miss Guest** *and* **Utterson** *go offstage.*

• •

SCENE 6

An evening, two months later. The hallway of Dr Jekyll's house and then his medical rooms.

Lights up on **Poole** *and* **Mrs Temple** *in the hall, who are happily organising the other servants,* **Tump** *and* **Housemaids 1** *and* **2.**

Poole	Fetch an umbrella, Tump, to see the gentlemen to their coaches.
Tump	Yes, sir. *[He goes offstage]*
Mrs Temple	Have the trolley ready to clear the table, girls. But you're not to start until the guests have gone.
Housemaid 1	Very good, Mrs Temple.
Housemaid 2	Yes, miss.

The **housemaids** *go offstage.*

Poole	It's gone well tonight, hasn't it?
Mrs Temple	The doctor and his friends have enjoyed themselves from start to finish.
Poole	A little different from when the doctor first moved in here.
Mrs Temple	He couldn't get through an evening without losing his temper then.
Poole	It's not really my place to say it. But he seems a changed man, these past two months. Spending all his time seeing to the sick.
Mrs Temple	He's not even paid, for a lot of the work.
Poole	He's back on good terms with his friends.
Mrs Temple	If you ask me, Sir Danvers' murder was a blessing in disguise; ridding him of that villainous Hyde.
Poole	I agree with you there, Mrs Temple.
Mrs Temple	Ever since then, the master's been a pleasure to work for. Even-tempered. Moderate in all things.
Poole	That he has.
Mrs Temple	In fact, tonight's the first time I've seen him drink brandy in ever so long.
Poole	Surely a man may relax amongst his friends, Mrs Temple?
Lanyon	*[Approaching from offstage]* A most enjoyable evening, Jekyll.
	Poole and **Mrs Temple** *fall silent, as* **Lanyon**, **Utterson** *and* **Jekyll** *come onstage.*
Utterson	You've been on sparkling form.
Jekyll	Not at all. I've simply reflected the dazzling lights, sitting either side of me.
Utterson	*[Amused]* My conversation dazzling? I believe you've drunk a little too deeply tonight, Jekyll.

Lanyon	We must all meet up again soon.
Jekyll	Call in whenever you wish. You are always most welcome.
	Tump hurries onstage with a large umbrella.
Tump	Here you are, gentlemen.
	Tump starts to put it up, when Jekyll stops him.
Jekyll	Put the umbrella up when the guests are outside, Tump.
Tump	Oh. Yes, sir.
Lanyon	*[Quietly to Utterson]* I haven't seen Jekyll so affable in a long time.
Utterson	*[Quietly]* Quite his old self again.
Jekyll	See to the door, Poole.
	Poole goes offstage to open the front door. Tump stands proudly poised to go out with the umbrella.
	A very good night to you, Lanyon.
Lanyon	*[Shaking Jekyll's hand]* Good night.
Jekyll	And you, my dear Utterson.
Utterson	*[Shaking Jekyll's hand. Quietly]* It does my heart good to see you so at ease with yourself again.
Poole	*[Comes back onstage. To Tump]* No need for the umbrella. The rain has passed over.
Tump	*[Disappointed. His big moment has gone]* Oh.
Lanyon	*[Going offstage]* Ah. My carriage is there.
Utterson	*[Going offstage]* Another fine meal, Mrs Temple.
Mrs Temple	Thank you, sir.
	Poole goes offstage to close the front door.
Jekyll	My friend is quite right, Mrs Temple. The chestnut soup was exquisite.

Mrs Temple	I'm pleased you liked it.
Jekyll	As for the jugged hare! You have surpassed yourself this evening.
Mrs Temple	I try to oblige, sir.
	Poole comes back onstage.
Poole	*[To Tump]* You can put that away now.
Tump	Yes, sir.
	Tump and Poole go offstage.
Mrs Temple	With your permission, I'll set the girls to clearing.
Jekyll	One thing more, Mrs Temple.
Mrs Temple	Yes, sir?
Jekyll	*[Slightly embarrassed]* If you hear… um… any movement in the night… You're not to be alarmed.
Mrs Temple	No, sir?
Jekyll	The house feels uncomfortably warm and sticky to me at the moment.
Mrs Temple	The effects of the brandy, I expect, sir.
Jekyll	And… um… now that the rain has passed, I may let myself out for a walk later on.
Mrs Temple	Oh. I see, sir.
Jekyll	So don't worry if you hear the door at the back open and close in the early hours. No need to rouse everyone against an intruder.
Mrs Temple	No, sir. I'll know it's just you. Taking the night air.
Jekyll	Quite so. Now, go and see to the girls.
Mrs Temple	Yes, sir. *[She goes offstage]*

Jekyll   *[To himself. Walking to his medical rooms]* Well, why not? For two months I've lived the life of a saint. Done nothing but set broken bones for families that cannot pay. Soothed racking coughs. Treated diphtheria. Reassured despairing mothers with kindness and good medicine. And I've enjoyed every moment. In a way. *[He goes up the steps to the upper level]* But tonight I mean to put myself first for once. Another side of me yearns to be let free. *[He points in mock accusation at the skeleton]* Don't look at me like that! I've no thought of bringing back Hyde. *[He takes down and puts on an overcoat hanging at the side of the cabinet]* I shall go out as myself. An ordinary, secret sinner once more.

*Lights down. **Jekyll** goes offstage.*

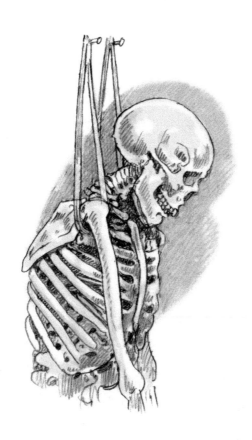

SCENE 7

The following morning. Mr Utterson's office.

Lights up on **Miss Guest,** *who is filing some documents.* **Utterson** *comes onstage.*

Utterson	I'm astonished, Miss Guest.
Miss Guest	Why's that, sir?
Utterson	You are alone for once. Where's your admirer?
Miss Guest	If you mean your cousin, Mr Enfield…
Utterson	Who else would I mean?
Miss Guest	He was here for a short time earlier. To confirm your walk together next week.
Utterson	Excellent. And then you sent him on his way, with your usual good sense?
Miss Guest	*[Shrugs non-committally]* Well…
Utterson	*[Not really listening]* Good, good. Now I apologise if I am a little late.
Miss Guest	Not at all, sir.
Utterson	But I slept more soundly than in a long time. I had an excellent evening's entertainment at Dr Jekyll's.
Miss Guest	How is the doctor?
Utterson	In fine spirits. He's a changed man since Hyde has gone. And those small doubts we had some weeks ago, Miss Guest.
Miss Guest	About the handwriting, sir?
Utterson	The resemblance between Hyde and Jekyll's. We need trouble ourselves no more, I fancy. Whether Jekyll wrote both items at the command of a murderer no longer matters. I am satisfied that Hyde is long clear of London.

Miss Guest	It's astonishing if he has got away, sir. The police have been watching every station and every port since the murder.
Utterson	As his letter showed, he was supremely confident of disappearing.
Miss Guest	Where do you think he's taking refuge?
Utterson	There may never be a satisfactory answer to that question. And in truth, I no longer care to know. As long he never returns to ruin Jekyll's life again.

Lights down. **Utterson** *and* **Miss Guest** *go offstage.*

SCENE 8

The same morning. A bench in a London park.

Lights up on a slightly hung over but happy **Jekyll,** *sitting on the bench. Birdsong.*

A **police constable** *walks past.*

Jekyll	Good morning, officer.
Constable	Morning, sir.
Jekyll	Lovely here, isn't it? Fresh air. Birdsong. Primroses coming through the grass.
Constable	Very nice, sir. *[He goes offstage]*
Jekyll	*[To himself]* A wonderful day to be alive. And I needn't feel guilty about last night… Dear Madame Cuvier… I just wish my head was clearer. Lucky that Lanyon wasn't at Cuvier's… Though what does it matter if I'm seen? Better to sin a little and do a great deal of good, than to have milkwater in your veins and do neither. *[He shudders, then rubs his brow]* That's better. Less cognac the next time perhaps. For there will be a next time. *[He shudders more powerfully]* Good Lord! *[He starts*

shaking and shuddering violently as he starts to transform. He groans as he battles to stay as Jekyll] No... no... Not here... I cannot!

He struggles to his feet. Looking round, terrified, he continues to violently transform, as he struggles offstage.

Lights down.

● ●

SCENE 9

Shortly after. Dr Lanyon's house. Lights up on the living room.

Lanyon *is reading a newspaper in his armchair when his butler,* **Jenkins,** *enters with a letter.*

Jenkins	A letter's arrived for you, sir.
Lanyon	*[Takes the letter]* I thought there was no more post today.
Jenkins	It was hand-delivered by a messenger boy. From a public house, I believe, sir. He wouldn't say who sent him.
Lanyon	*[Opening the letter]* The letter's from Dr Jekyll. I recognise the hand.
Jenkins	Any reply, sir?
Lanyon	Wait a moment. *[Starts reading it. To himself]* Good heavens! He must be falling back into his old, fanciful ways. *[To Jenkins]* Have the carriage brought round, Jenkins.
Jenkins	You mean to go out again, sir?
Lanyon	I have no choice. My friend begs me to collect certain items from his medical rooms and bring them back here.
Jenkins	Is he ill, sir?
Lanyon	Some kind of brain fever, if you want my diagnosis. None of his requests make any sense. I'd ignore them, but he seems so desperate. *[Checking the letter]* And it gets worse. He says a visitor will come to collect the chemicals late tonight. Oh! This is madness!

Jenkins	Sir?
Lanyon	*[Making a decision]* Well. He is a friend, when all is said and done. *[To **Jenkins**]* You and the rest of the staff may finish your duties two hours early tonight, Jenkins.
Jenkins	*[Surprised]* Thank you, sir.
Lanyon	Apparently my visitor doesn't care to be seen by anyone. Except me.
	*Lights down. **Lanyon** and **Jenkins** go offstage.*

SCENE 10

	Late that evening. Dr Lanyon's house. There is a hammering on the front door through the darkness.
Lanyon	*[Offstage, through darkness]* Have patience, man! Patience.
	Lights up on the living room, as the bolts on the front door are drawn back offstage.
Hyde	*[Offstage]* Have you got it?
Lanyon	*[Offstage]* Be so good as to step through.
	The front door is closed offstage.
Hyde	*[Hurries onstage]* Have you got it? The chemicals Dr Jekyll asked you to collect?
Lanyon	*[Coming onstage with a small drawer]* I have the drawer from his medical cabinet.
Hyde	*[Desperate]* Give it to me.
Lanyon	Sir, you are forgetting your manners.
Hyde	*[With a great effort]* I beg your pardon, Dr Lanyon. My impatience has driven out my politeness. But your friend, Dr Jekyll, is very keen that I should have the contents of the drawer as soon as possible.

Lanyon	Then you may have them.

He passes the drawer over. **Hyde** *cries out with relief as, in a frenzy, he starts taking the contents out.*

Compose yourself, man.

Hyde	*[Trying to smile politely]* Have you a measuring glass I can use, Doctor?
Lanyon	*[Going to collect one]* Yes. I can let you have that.
Hyde	Oh very good. Very, very good.
Lanyon	*[Offering the glass]* Will this do?
Hyde	Oh yes, it's excellent. Most excellent.

Hyde *pours powder and a phial of liquid from the drawer into the glass.*

[Muttering to himself] Yes, yes. That's it.

He looks in satisfaction at the glass, then turns to **Lanyon.**

Now, will you be guided by me, Dr Lanyon? Will you let me leave with this? Or has your curiosity got the better of you? Think before you answer, because I'll do whatever you say. If I leave, you will have helped a friend who was in mortal distress. But you'll be no richer or wiser than before. If you tell me to stay, you will see sights that would stagger Satan himself. A whole new kingdom of knowledge will appear in this room. New paths to fame and power will lie open before you. So which is it to be?

Lanyon	*[Intrigued]* I have gone too far in this matter without explanation already. You may stay and carry on with whatever you are about.
Hyde	Good. But remember your vows as a doctor. While I'm alive, you can never tell anyone what you're about to witness.
Lanyon	Very well.
Hyde	And now – behold!

Hyde *drains the glass as the lights come down.*

SCENE 11

A week later. A street near Dr Lanyon's house.

Lights up on **Enfield** *and* **Utterson.**

Utterson	I find it completely inexplicable.
Enfield	The change in Jekyll's mood?
Utterson	It's extraordinary. Up to a week ago, he couldn't have been more sociable. He told Lanyon and myself to call in on him whenever we wished. Quite like the old days.
Enfield	But since then?
Utterson	Whenever I try to see him, I am sent away without explanation. Other than, 'Dr Jekyll is too busy to receive visitors.'
Enficld	Perhaps he is.
Utterson	Even if he is overwhelmed with patients, I would expect him to see me for a few moments. He was so insistent that I call on him again.
Enfield	What do you think's happened?
Utterson	I fear he may have dropped into his old, unfortunate habits. Forsaking friendship for experiment and letting it darken his mind. That's why I suggested we walk towards Dr Lanyon's house.
Enfield	Ah.
Utterson	I mean to ask Lanyon if he has any explanation for Jekyll's changed behaviour.
Enfield	If you're going to be busy with Lanyon, I'll say farewell here and take the opportunity to call by your offices.
Utterson	*[Gently]* You know you're making rather a nuisance of yourself to Miss Guest?

Enfield	Perhaps in the past, Gabriel. But I hope Sarah feels a little differently now.
Utterson	Oh. She's told you her name?
Enfield	And has agreed to be my companion at my friend Gray's wedding.
Utterson	Richard, don't take this amiss. But I have a very high regard for Miss Guest. I would not see her hurt by anyone.
Enfield	I will not hurt her.
Utterson	So you say. But life has treated her harshly in the past and driven her into actions which... *[Considers what to say carefully]*... She is more vulnerable than you might imagine.
Enfield	I know. She has told me a little of her upbringing.
Utterson	*[Surprised]* Has she?
Enfield	Quite something to have been considered the smartest pick-pocket in the whole of Charing Cross.
Utterson	She was forced into it by a villainous uncle.
Enfield	Until you appeared, as her saviour.
Utterson	Her saviour? Not at all.
Enfield	That is how she sees you.
Utterson	Nonsense! She always had great gifts for learning. I merely recognised her ability, when a case brought me into contact with her family.
Enfield	You gave her an opportunity to better herself.
Utterson	And, my word, how she seized it. The credit is all hers.
Enfield	She is indeed a jewel of a woman. Which is why I don't give a jot for her past.
Utterson	*[Impressed]* Good for you.
Enfield	My only aim now is to make her future considerably kinder. *[Moving off]* Good day, Gabriel.

Utterson	*[Smiles]* Good day, Richard.
	Lights down. **Enfield** *and* **Utterson** *go offstage.*

• •

SCENE 12

At the same time. Dr Jekyll's medical rooms.

Lights up on the steps to the upper level. The door at the top is closed.

Poole *comes onstage hesitantly and lays a packet of chemical salts on the top step. He knocks on the door.*

Poole	*[Calls through door]* It's here, sir. The salts from the chemists on Waterloo Road.

There's no reply. **Poole** *walks slowly down the steps, then waits and watches secretly.*

The door at the top opens slightly. **Hyde's** *hand reaches round, feels for the packet of salts, then takes them in, before slamming the door shut.*

Horrified, **Poole** *goes offstage.*

Lights down.

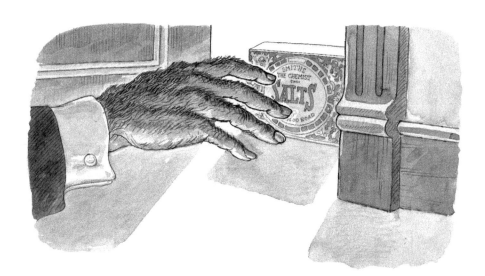

SCENE 13

A few moments later. Dr Lanyon's house.

*Lights up on a very ill **Lanyon**, sitting and talking to **Utterson**.*

| Lanyon | I have days left, Utterson. Weeks at most. |

Utterson   My dear fellow. I had no idea. Can nothing be done for you?

Lanyon   Nothing. I suffered such a seizure a week ago, I know I cannot recover. Well, I can't complain. Life has been pleasant. Or it used to be. If I had realised what horrors it contains, I might have been glad to leave sooner.

Utterson   My dear Lanyon. This is sad news. It comes as a second blow to me. I fear Jekyll has fallen ill too. Has he visited you?

Lanyon   *[Agitated]* Don't speak of that man! Never, I beg you, Utterson!

Utterson   Why not?

Lanyon   It is through him I am suffering like this.

Utterson   How is that possible?

Lanyon shakes his head. He doesn't want to speak.

This is a most serious claim to make against an old friend. Can you substantiate it, Lanyon?

Lanyon   I am bound by the Hippocratic oath[1] to remain silent. *[He becomes increasingly agitated]* But I cannot forget what I have seen. Such awful, dreadful sights. *[Distressed]* My foolish curiosity has brought me to this!

Utterson   *[Goes over to calm him]* Compose yourself, my dear fellow.

Lanyon   *[Distraught]* I see him still! I see him!

---

1 The Hippocratic oath is a solemn promise made by doctors to treat their patients fairly. It is named after Hippocrates, a great physician, who is considered the father of western medicine.

Utterson	Lanyon! Forget that I said anything of Jekyll.
Lanyon	I cannot! I wish to God I could, but I cannot!

Jenkins enters.

Jenkins	There is a visitor, Dr Lanyon.
Utterson	Send him away, man! Can't you see your master is in no condition to receive anyone.
Jenkins	He won't be sent away, sir. I believe it is you he wishes to see.
Utterson	Me?

Poole comes in, highly distressed.

Poole	Mr Utterson, I was told at your offices you were here. I beg you to come with me at once.
Utterson	Why?
Poole	Something is very wrong with Dr Jekyll. I believe he is beyond all help, unless it is yours.
Lanyon	Don't go to him, Utterson. Spare yourself what I have suffered.
Poole	We have no one else to turn to, except you, sir.
Lanyon	I beg you, Utterson. Don't!
Utterson	I can't ignore the need of another friend in crisis. Very well, Poole.
Poole	*[Heartfelt]* Thank you, sir. Thank you. We must make haste. *[He hurries offstage]*
Utterson	Goodbye Lanyon. *[To Jenkins, as he hurries offstage]* See to your master.

Lights down. Lanyon and Jenkins go offstage.

Moments later. Dr Jekyll's medical rooms.

*Lights up, on **Jekyll**, who is writing at the table on the lower level. As he writes, he struggles to stop himself transforming into **Hyde** again.*

Jekyll

[*Writing*] I only have a few moments left, so this will be my final record. I want the world to understand what lies beyond the door I have so violently wrenched open with my transformational elixir. I cannot adequately express the grinding pain in the bones and the nausea I felt in my first transformation. Nor the incredible sweetness of becoming Mr Edward Hyde for the first time. I felt instantly younger, lighter, happier in body. Untroubled by any complaint of conscience. I swelled with pride in proving my doubters, like Lanyon and Carew, completely wrong.

He shudders and has to stop and breathe deeply to control himself, before resuming.

So successful was the separation and so independent was Mr Hyde, that I set him up in his own lodgings. After an unfortunate incident with a match-girl, I also gave him a bank account and ensured, by way of a will, that he would have the means to thrive, if anything untoward happened to me.

He shudders again, before resuming.

At first, I was surprised to note that Hyde was smaller and less fully formed than myself. I reasoned it was because the more animal side of my nature, from which he sprang, was also less developed. But the more licence I gave him, the more robust he became, until, on one occasion, he released himself from my sleeping form, despite my having taken no potion at all. My blood chilled to ice when I woke to see his hand on the coverlet of the bed. After transforming back into my own shape, I went a full ten days without attempting to change again, before convincing myself it had only been an unfortunate mischance. Would that I never had! My devil had been too long caged and came out roaring.

*He cries out in pain, as he struggles to stay as **Jekyll**.*

I must be brief. After I released Hyde, only for him to murder Sir Danvers Carew, I swore I would never touch the cursed mixture again. I have kept my word. For two months, I devoted myself only to my work and the company of good friends. But then I lapsed. One night, I fell into my old pleasure-seeking habits – as myself, not Hyde. But this loosening of my self-control is all Hyde needed. He seized command of me once more in a public park. If I had fled home, my servants would have had me arrested for Carew's murder at once. Instead, I hid in the lowest of taverns for a day, before my friend Lanyon's kindness allowed me to escape back into my own form... How I regret the shock I gave him, when he witnessed my transformation. I fear it has caused him irreparable harm.

He cries out again, as the pain increases.

And now my own suffering is almost complete. I have run out of the original batch of salts I used for the transformational mixture. I took the last of it just now, but cannot hold Hyde at bay for much longer. Despite trying every wholesale chemist in London, I cannot find a new batch that will work. I am driven to conclude there must have been some impurity in the original, which proved essential to the process, but which cannot be replaced. Now both parts of me are caught in a living hell.

He struggles desperately, as he starts to transform during the following.

My other half has almost gained complete dominion over me. The thought of permanently being Hyde is unbearable to me. Yet, he also lives in terror – of being caught and hanged as a murderer. Perhaps his fear of the gallows will make him a self-destroyer. I cannot answer for him. All I know – these are my last seconds as Dr Henry Jekyll and I have only one last regret to pass on, before my unhappy life comes to an end...

*Choking and struggling, he scratches out a few more words to complete his letter, then transforms once more into **Hyde**.*

Poole	*[Offstage]* It's very good of you, sir. We live in fear that something terrible has happened.

*Terrified by the voices, **Hyde** runs up the steps to the upper level, closes and locks the door at the top.*

Utterson	*[Coming onstage]* He has locked himself away?
Poole	We haven't seen the doctor for the best part of a week, sir. But he leaves notes – sending me to this chemist, then another, then another. Whenever I return with salts, I leave them on the steps. Soon after, there is always a howling of despair from up there, as though his heart is broke.
Utterson	Well, well. Knock and let him know I am here.
Poole	*[Goes up the steps and knocks on the door]* Mr Utterson has called by, sir.
Hyde	*[Calls from behind the door]* Tell him I cannot see anyone.
Poole	Very well, sir. *[Comes down the steps. To **Utterson**]* That wasn't my master's voice, was it, sir?
Utterson	*[Anxious]* It seems very much changed.
Mrs Temple	*[Coming onstage]* It is more than changed, Mr Utterson. Say what you have seen Mr Poole.
Utterson	Well?
Poole	Before I came to find you, sir, I had left a last packet of salts on the steps. Normally I wouldn't take such a liberty, but this time, I was so worried for the master, I waited and watched. The door opened and a hand reached down to take them.
Mrs Temple	Tell him, Mr Poole.
Poole	It was not Dr Jekyll's hand. It was Hyde's.
Mrs Temple	The murderer's come back and done away with the master.

Utterson	That's presuming too much. We don't know where Dr Jekyll is.
Poole	*[Points to the upper level]* He's in there, sir. We have watched and waited for him to leave these past few days. And he never has.
Utterson	He may have let himself out through the back way.
Mrs Temple	No, sir. *[She brandishes a broken key]* We found the key, broken in the lock, two days ago. No one can leave that way any more.
Poole	There's only one place Dr Jekyll can be, sir. *[He points to the upper level again]* In there. At the mercy of that monster.
Utterson	Then I must go in.
Poole	You can't, sir. He keeps the door locked.
Utterson	*[To **Mrs Temple**]* Fetch Bradshaw. Tell him to bring something we may force it with.
Mrs Temple	Sir. *[She hurries offstage]*
Utterson	If it is Hyde up there …
Poole	*[Cuts in]* You heard him speak, sir. You know that isn't the doctor.
Utterson	I fear you are right. Then we must make sure he cannot escape.
Poole	I'll help you, sir. No man alone is a match for that devil.

Utterson	Well said.
	They stand at the bottom of the steps. **Hyde** *lets out a scream of despair from behind the door.*
	Dear God! *[Calls]* Do you have Jekyll in there? Release him, or you will answer for your actions!
	Bradshaw, *carrying a mallet and chisel, comes onstage with* **Mrs Temple** *and* **Tump**.
Bradshaw	*[Holding up the tools]* These should do, sir.
Utterson	Are you bold enough to force the door?
Bradshaw	Sir.
Poole	We think Hyde's done some violence to the master up there.
	Bradshaw *goes up to the door.*
Utterson	Stand away, Mrs Temple. Tump, Poole, prepare yourselves.
	Bradshaw *strikes the lock with the chisel. The door swings open. The dead body of* **Hyde** *tumbles down the steps.*
	Utterson *approaches the body cautiously, then kneels down and sniffs.*
	The smell of almonds. He has used cyanide to kill himself.
Mrs Temple	Is the master there, sir?
Utterson	*[Stands up and looks through the door]* I can't see him. And this creature can't tell us what he's done with him. Look around for any sign of what's happened to Dr Jekyll.
	Lanyon *comes onstage, helped by* **Jenkins**.
Lanyon	If you have Hyde there, you won't find Jekyll.
Utterson	*[Coming down the steps]* Lanyon, you're risking your health, coming here.
Lanyon	In the hope I could spare you what I have suffered. And now that he is dead, I am free to speak. You won't find Jekyll.

Utterson	What do you mean?
Lanyon	[Pointing to **Hyde**] This vile object and our friend are one and the same.
Utterson	[Staggered] What?
Mrs Temple	[Quietly to **Jenkins**] Take him home. Your master's wits are wandering.
Lanyon	What I say is true. [He sits down by the table] That is what I saw, when Hyde drank off the potion he had mixed up. He staggered, stared, gasped with an open mouth. My whole mind was struck with terror as he became Henry Jekyll.
Poole	Impossible, sir.
Lanyon	But true.
Tump	[Holds up Jekyll's letter to show **Utterson**] Sir. This is addressed to you.
Utterson	[Takes it] Thank you. [He scans through it]
Mrs Temple	The master and Mr Hyde, one and the same?
Lanyon	I fear so.
Poole	The world must be torn inside out, for such wonders to happen.
Bradshaw	[To **Utterson**] It's not possible, is it, sir?
Utterson	[Looks up] Not merely possible. But it has happened. Something of Henry Jekyll must lie within Hyde's corpse. [To **Poole**] Take it to a bedroom or somewhere more fitting.
Poole	Sir. [He signals **Tump** and **Bradshaw** to help him]
Utterson	Help them, Mrs Temple.
Mrs Temple	Sir. [Goes to help the others]
Utterson	[To the servants] When you return, the cabinet and all its contents must be broken up.
Poole	They will be, sir.

*[He helps the other servants carry **Hyde** offstage]*

Utterson	*[Indicating the letter]* Jekyll describes here each step he took to overturn nature.
Lanyon	The method must not be made public.
Utterson	It never shall be, lest others try to follow his path and release their own darkest desires.
Lanyon	The world would become hellish.
Utterson	It shall not happen! And yet… *[Glances at the letter]* poor Jekyll closes his letter with a lament for what might have been, in other circumstances. *[Reads]* 'If, when I first drank the mixture, my mind had been full of generous thoughts, the result might have been entirely different…'
Jekyll	*[Offstage. Ethereal]*…since the drug did not discriminate between the different sides of a person. Whatever it found uppermost, it set free. At the time I took it, my virtuous side slept, while the evil in me was awake and alert. It seized its opportunity and thus appeared Edward Hyde. But as I leave this world, my last, tormenting thought is that, at another, better time, an angel might have come forth in place of that fiend.
Utterson	A fiend indeed. *[Puts the letter down]* Oh, poor Jekyll.

***Poole, Mrs Temple, Tump** and **Bradshaw** return.*

Poole	Sir?
Utterson	*[Points to the upper level]* Destroy it all!

Blackout.

ACTIVITIES

Framework Substrand	Activities						
	1	2	3	4	5	6	7
1.1 Developing active listening skills and strategies		✓	✓		✓	✓	
1.2 Understanding and responding to what speakers say in formal and informal contexts		✓	✓		✓	✓	
2.1 Developing and adapting speaking skills and strategies in formal and informal contexts	✓	✓	✓		✓	✓	
2.2 Using and adapting the conventions and forms of spoken texts		✓	✓			✓	
3.1 Developing and adapting discussion skills and strategies in formal and informal contexts	✓		✓		✓	✓	
3.2 Taking roles in group discussion		✓	✓		✓		
4.1 Using different dramatic approaches to explore ideas, texts and issues			✓	✓	✓		
4.2 Developing, adapting and responding to dramatic techniques, conventions and styles			✓	✓	✓		
5.1 Developing and adapting active reading skills and strategies	✓	✓					✓
5.2 Understanding and responding to ideas, viewpoints, themes and purposes in texts	✓	✓	✓	✓		✓	
5.3 Reading and engaging with a wide and varied range of texts						✓	
6.1 Relating texts to the social, historical and cultural contexts in which they were written		✓					✓
6.2 Analysing how writers' use of linguistic and literary features shapes and influences meaning	✓						✓
6.3 Analysing writers' use of organisation, structure, layout and presentation		✓		✓			
7.1 Generating ideas, planning and drafting				✓		✓	
7.2 Using and adapting the conventions and forms of texts on paper and on screen				✓		✓	
8.1 Developing viewpoint, voice and ideas				✓		✓	
8.2 Varying sentences and punctuation for clarity and effect				✓			
8.3 Improving vocabulary for precision and impact	✓					✓	✓
8.4 Developing varied linguistic and literary techniques							✓
8.5 Structuring, organising and presenting texts in a variety of forms on paper and on screen	✓			✓		✓	
8.6 Developing and using editing and proofreading skills on paper and on screen				✓		✓	
9.1 Using the conventions of standard English						✓	✓
9.2 Using grammar accurately and appropriately						✓	
9.3 Reviewing spelling and increasing knowledge of word derivations, patterns and families	✓					✓	
10.1 Exploring language variation and development according to time, place, culture, society and technology							✓
10.2 Commenting on language use							✓

1   THE GOOD AND THE BAD

Dr Jekyll tells his friends that he is working on 'dissecting the human mind'. He is trying to 'tear apart the different sides of a man's personality. The good from the bad. The cowardly from the brave'.

GLOSSARY

Dissecting means cutting something up in order to examine it.

The word comes from two Latin words:

dis = apart

sectum = cut

---

1. Think about your own personality. How would you dissect it into good and bad? Write down two of your 'good' qualities and two of your 'bad' qualities. For example:

Good	Bad
friendly	jealous
funny	moody

2. Share your lists as a class. Add as many different adjectives as you can to describe aspects of people's personalities. Here are some to start you off:

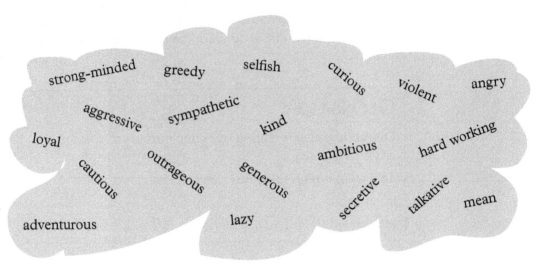

strong-minded greedy selfish curious violent angry
aggressive sympathetic kind
loyal ambitious hard working
cautious outrageous generous secretive talkative mean
adventurous lazy

3. Display your results as a Venn diagram. Qualities that could be either 'good' or 'bad' should go in the middle section.

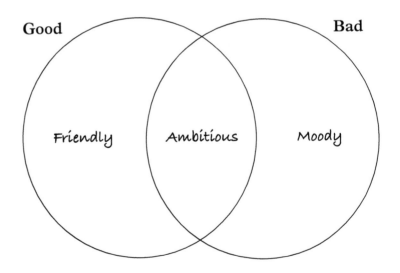

Good   **Bad**

Friendly   Ambitious   Moody

4. Draw and cut out a large outline of a person. Stick it on the wall and draw a line down the middle from head to feet. Label one side 'Dr Jekyll' and the other side 'Mr Hyde'.

In pairs, skim the playscript and find an event that shows something about the character of Dr Jekyll or Mr Hyde. Jot down what it shows on a sticky note and stick it on the relevant side of the outline. Take turns to explain your notes to the class.

Here are some events that you might look at:

Mr Hyde meets Utterson (Act 1 Scene 8)

Hyde's encounter with Ann Manning (Act 1 Scene 4)

Dr Jekyll's letter (Act 2 Scene 14)

Jekyll talking to his mirror image (Act 1 Scene 11)

The party at Jekyll's new home (Act 1 Scene 1)

Hyde murders Carew (Act 1 Scene 12)

Hyde reveals his secret to Lanyon (Act 2 Scene 10)

Hyde escapes (Act 2 Scene 2)

Jekyll talks with friends and servants (Act 2 Scene 6)

ASSESSMENT

● **Self-assessment.** Rate yourself out of three (with three being the highest score) on how well you did the following:
  • described your own personality
  • worked with a group to complete the Venn diagram.

● **Peer assessment.** Ask your group to comment on two good aspects of your explanation of your sticky notes, and one aspect that could be improved.

2 SEQUENCING AND SUMMARISING

Imagine you are the director of a theatre company. You have decided to stage a production of *Jekyll and Hyde* and you are meeting your actors to introduce them to the play.

You have two main tasks:

- to summarise the story
- to give them some background about the author and historical setting.

1. You have prepared a storyboard for the play, with different events on different sheets of paper to be lined up or flipped through. However, the sheets have got muddled up.

   Sort the sheets into the correct order and be prepared to explain the sequence of events. You may work in pairs on this task.

A

Utterson reads Dr Jekyll's last letter.

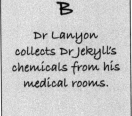

B

Dr Lanyon collects Dr Jekyll's chemicals from his medical rooms.

C

Mr Hyde attacks Ann Manning.

D

Mr Hyde transforms in front of Dr Lanyon.

E

Mr Hyde murders Sir Danvers Carew.

F

Pool and Utterson break down Dr Jekyll's door.

G

Dr Jekyll invites his friends to his new house.

H

Utterson meets Mr Hyde.

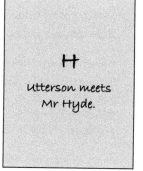

2. The author of the original novel was Robert Louis Stevenson. He wrote *The Strange Case of Dr Jekyll and Mr Hyde* in 1885.

Here are some historical facts:

> In 1859 Charles Darwin published a book called *Origin of Species*, which explained how people had descended from apes. Many people were shocked at the thought that they were related to animals.

Stevenson came from a religious family with strict rules about behaviour. However, when he was a student Stevenson used to go into town, disguised as another character, to drink, socialise and behave badly.

As a boy, Stevenson was fascinated by the true story of Deacon Brodie who was a respected furniture-maker by day but a robber by night.

Write some notes about how these facts may have influenced Stevenson's story.

Darwin's idea that people descended from apes influenced Stevenson because Hyde is described as...

Stevenson liked pretending to be someone else when he wanted more freedom. He used this idea in his novel by...

The true story of Deacon Brodie is echoed in Jekyll and Hyde because...

3. In your role as director, present a summary of the story of *Jekyll and Hyde* to your actors (the rest of the group or class). Then give them some background information about what may have given Stevenson ideas for his novel.

ASSESSMENT

● **Self-assessment.** How well do you understand the sequence of events in the playscript? Choose between:
  ● not very well
  ● well enough to know roughly what happens
  ● very well.

● **Peer assessment.** Ask your group or class to give you two positive comments about how well you introduced the story of *Jekyll and Hyde* to them. Ask them to suggest one way that you could improve on your presentation.

3   BRINGING A CHARACTER TO LIFE

Image you are putting on a production of this play. The director wants one actor to play both Dr Jekyll and Mr Hyde. He or she has asked three members of the team to work out how best to do this.

In groups of three, take on the roles of:
- sound and lighting manager
- costume and props manager
- voice and movement coach.

1. First, work together to think of as many ideas as you can. You may find it useful to jot them down in three spider diagrams. For example:

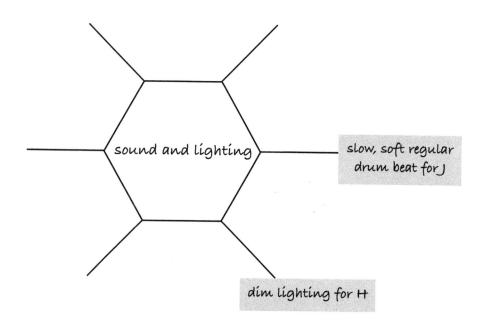

sound and lighting

slow, soft regular drum beat for J

dim lighting for H

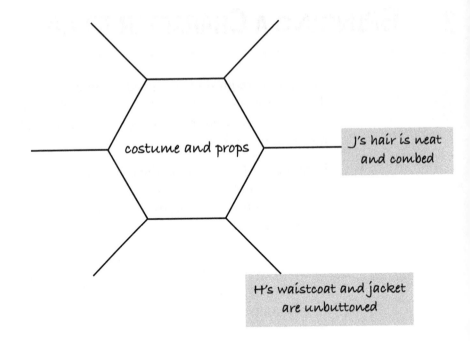

costume and props

J's hair is neat
and combed

H's waistcoat and jacket
are unbuttoned

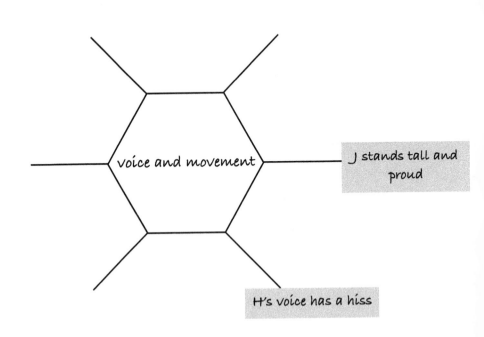

voice and movement

J stands tall and
proud

H's voice has a hiss

2. Next, each person works in detail on their area of expertise. They have to:
   - choose the ideas that they think will work best
   - work out the detail of these ideas
   - write some notes to help explain them to the director.

> **Remember**
> You need to make it clear to the audience whether they are watching Dr Jekyll or Mr Hyde. There won't be time for big costume changes, so one actor has to change 'personality' in front of the audience.

Here are some quotations from the play that may help you with some ideas.

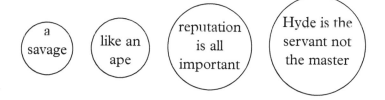

a savage | like an ape | reputation is all important | Hyde is the servant not the master

Think carefully about how other villains and heroes are depicted – on stage or in films. For example, the Joker in *The Dark Knight*; Clark Kent in *Superman*.
- How do they stand and walk?
- What sort of voice do they have?
- What are their facial expressions?
- Do we see them clearly or in dim lighting?
- What sort of music or sounds are in the background?

3. In your groups of three, rehearse a short presentation to give to your director. Work out what you are going to say and demonstrate your ideas (for example, to show how Hyde should walk and speak). If possible, gather together a few props or examples of costume.

4. Present your ideas to your director (teacher). The rest of the class can listen in, as if they are also members of the theatre group.

5. Invite questions from your audience and be prepared to develop your ideas further if you are given helpful suggestions.

ASSESSMENT

● **Self-assessment.** Think carefully about how well you worked in your group. Give yourself a thumbs up 👍 or thumbs down 👎 as to whether you did the following:
  ● suggested ideas for the spider diagrams
  ● listened to others' ideas
  ● gave help and advice during the rehearsal.

● **Teacher assessment.** Ask your teacher to comment on two things that you did well in your presentation and one thing that you could improve.

4 EXTENDING A SCENE

Act 2 Scene 10 ends with Mr Hyde drinking the mix of powder and liquid in front of Dr Lanyon.

What happens next is described in Robert Louis Stevenson's novel:

> He put the glass to his lips and drank at one gulp. A cry followed; he reeled, staggered, clutched at the table and held on, staring with injected eyes, gasping with open mouth; and as I looked there came, I thought, a change—he seemed to swell—his face became suddenly black and the features seemed to melt and alter—and the next moment, I had sprung to my feet and leaped back against the wall, my arm raised to shield me from that prodigy, my mind submerged in terror.
>
> 'O God!' I screamed, and 'O God!' again and again; for there before my eyes—pale and shaken, and half fainting, and groping before him with his hands, like a man restored from death—there stood Henry Jekyll!
>
> What he told me in the next hour, I cannot bring my mind to set on paper. I saw what I saw, I heard what I heard, and my soul sickened at it; and yet now when that sight has faded from my eyes, I ask myself if I believe it, and I cannot answer.

GLOSSARY

reeled	lurched backwards
injected	swollen, enlarged
prodigy	amazing thing
submerged	completely covered

1. With a partner, write more script (dialogue) for this scene.

    Think carefully about the conventions of writing script. Remember:
    - stage directions should be in brackets (or italics if you are using a word processor).
    - the name of the speaker is on the left.
    - what is said is direct speech, i.e. the exact words that are spoken.
    - the characters take turns to speak, responding to each other's words and actions.

TIPS FOR DIALOGUE

Dr Lanyon may be full of questions.

Dr Jekyll may be proud of his achievement.

Lanyon may feel upset/frightened/shocked/angry/curious.

Jekyll may want Lanyon to try out his potion.

Lanyon may be tempted.

Jekyll might be cross with Lanyon for not being more adventurous.

People who are shocked or frightened may use repetition, take long pauses, start lots of sentences but not finish them, etc.

2. When your script is finished, read it through, each taking one part. If some bits sound unconvincing, try to improve them.

3. Work out how you might stage this part of the scene, e.g. Mr Hyde/Dr Jekyll might have his back towards the audience during the transformation, so the audience just sees Dr Lanyon's reaction.
   - Think carefully about how the lines might be spoken (tone of voice, fast/slow, loudly or softly).
   - Decide what gestures each character might make and what their facial expressions might be.
   - Act out your new scene in front of an audience.

ASSESSMENT

- **Self-assessment.** Look at your new script. Give yourself a mark out of three for each of the following (three being the highest):
  - how well you used the information from the novel
  - how well you worked with your partner
  - how carefully you checked your script and improved it.

- **Peer assessment.** Ask the class for feedback on your new scene. Invite them to comment on what they thought was most effective and what they thought was least effective.

5   FREEZE FRAMES

In pairs or small groups, present freeze frames to the rest of the class, who have to guess which moments in the play are being shown.

To prepare for this activity:

> Choose three moments in the play to freeze frame.

↓

> Decide who will play which character in the frame.

↓

> Arrange the characters as if they have been frozen in the middle of a performance. (Think about how they might stand or sit, their expressions, gestures, eye contact with each other, whether they are speaking, etc.)

↓

> Each character must think carefully about their mood and how to convey that through their body language. They should think carefully about what they are thinking and feeling at that moment. (They may be questioned.)

↓

> Present your freeze frames. Allow time for a member of the audience to tap one character on the shoulder to hear his or her thoughts and feelings. (The character cannot mention any names.)

↓

> The class has to guess the moment in the play, name the characters taking part, and describe what is being shown. They should also explain what happened immediately after the scene being shown.

PROPS

You may use no more than one prop per scene, e.g. a letter, key, chair, tray or walking stick.

ASSESSMENT

- **Self-assessment.** Think about how you worked in the group. Give yourself a thumbs up 👍 or thumbs down 👎 for each of the following:
  - how well you contributed to the group's choices of scene
  - how well you listened to other people's ideas
  - how well you held your role in the freeze frame.

- **Peer assessment.** Ask the class for feedback on your freeze frames. Ask them to comment on what you did well. Then ask for suggestions as to how you could improve your frames. Invite students to demonstrate their ideas by swapping roles (i.e. they come to the 'stage' to show exactly what they mean).

6 PUBLICITY ONLINE

Imagine you work for an online company that advertises and sells tickets for theatre performances. You and a partner have been asked to promote a production of *The Strange Case of Dr Jekyll and Mr Hyde*.

Your task is to:
- design an image to advertise the play on the website
- write some text for the website to introduce the play
- make a 10-second film to promote the play.

DESIGN AN IMAGE

1. First, look at websites that promote theatre productions to give you some ideas.

2. Sketch out your own ideas, using different graphics, fonts and colours.

3. Show them to other people and take feedback.

4. Decide on the best image and work it into a final product. This could be hand-drawn and then photographed to go on the website, or you could design it using an electronic design package.

Remember
- Simple images often have most impact.
- Try to reflect the overall mood of the play.
- Make sure the title is clear.
- The image should be eye-catching, memorable and link to one of the themes of the play.

WRITING TEXT FOR THE WEBSITE

1. The first paragraph should give the title, the playwright's name and refer to the original novel and author.

2. The second paragraph should give a brief summary of the play (without giving away the ending). Try to make it sound exciting and dramatic, and to arouse the reader's curiosity.

3. The third paragraph should suggest a suitable audience, in terms of age.

4. Draft your copy, then give it to a partner. Ask them to suggest any improvements and to proofread for spelling or punctuation errors.

5. Write out your final text, if possible using a computer.

MAKE A 10-SECOND VIDEO

Use a mobile phone to record a short video of yourself or a partner, talking about what makes *Jekyll and Hyde* such a good play.

1. Think about the setting or background for your video. For example, should it be plain or include images? Should it be light or dark?

2. Will you include some background music?

3. Rehearse what you are going to say. Remember to keep it short and to the point.

4. Be enthusiastic about the play – you are trying to persuade people to go and see it!

ASSESSMENT

- **Self-assessment.** Give yourself marks out of five for the following (five being the highest):
  - how well you listened to your partner and talked about their ideas
  - how well you responded to the feedback you got
  - how carefully you finalised your work.

- **Teacher assessment.** Ask your teacher to judge which pair has produced the best publicity material for the play. He or she could select a winner for each category, i.e. the image, website text and video.

7 A HISTORICAL SETTING

The story of *Jekyll and Hyde* is set in the city of London, during the reign of Queen Victoria (1837 to 1901).

The playwright shows us the historical setting in:
- the variety of characters included in the play
- the way that the characters talk
- references to life in Victorian times.

CHARACTERS

1. Look at the list of characters in the play on pages 12 and 13. Which characters are unlikely to be in a play set in modern times? (There are six.)

2. In pairs, discuss what each of these characters did. If necessary, do some research to find out.

LANGUAGE

Here are some of the words and phrases used by characters in the play:

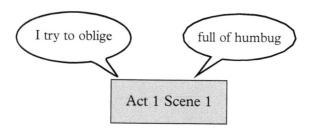

I try to oblige

full of humbug

Act 1 Scene 1

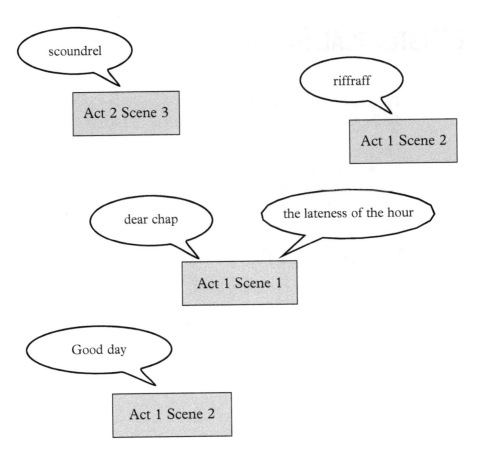

1. Look at the context in which these words are said. Write down how we might say similar things today, in modern language.

2. Find at least four more words and phrases in the playscript that we do not generally use today. Note them down and work out what they mean, or how we might say something similar today.

LIFE IN VICTORIAN LONDON

There are many references to life in Victorian times. Here are some, with their definitions, but they have got muddled up. Match up the correct pairs.

References

‘a gin palace’

‘peelers’

‘smelling salts’

‘sparrow grass’

to put someone ‘at the end of a rope’

Definitions

to hang someone

a luxurious bar selling gin and other alcoholic drinks

the first police force, set up by Sir Robert Peel

chemicals used to revive people who felt faint

an informal name for the vegetable ‘asparagus’

ASSESSMENT

- **Self-assessment.** Think carefully about whether you were ‘good’, ‘OK’ or ‘not very good’ at the following:
  - identifying the characters that wouldn’t have a role in a modern play
  - working out what words mean by their context (where they appear)
  - matching historical references to their definitions.

- **Peer assessment.** As a group, share your ideas about the modern equivalent of words and phrases used in the playscript. Decide which are the most accurate.

FURTHER ACTIVITIES

1. Hot-seat the character of Dr Jekyll and then Mr Hyde. Explore their feelings about what they did. Can they justify their actions?

2. Write a short newspaper article reporting the death of Sir Danvers Carew. Include a heading, a summary of events and some quotations by witnesses and the police.

3. Write three short text messages that Jekyll or Hyde might have sent to three separate people during the course of events in the play. Ask a partner to guess who they would have been sent to and at what point in the play.

4. The author of the novel, Robert Louis Stevenson, wrote other famous stories. Find out what they were and how successful he was as a writer. You might want to use the Internet or reference books for your research. Write one paragraph about his other works, and one paragraph about his overall success as a writer.

5. Hold a debate about whether Jekyll was right to experiment with separating out his 'primitive instincts' from his 'rational mind'. Can most research be justified if it gives us more understanding of ourselves and the world around us?